Kew PALACE

Kew PALACE

The OFFICIAL *Illustrated* HISTORY

SUSANNE GROOM and LEE PROSSER

Historic Royal
PALACES

in association with

MERRELL
LONDON · NEW YORK

Kew PALACE

The OFFICIAL Illustrated HISTORY

CONTENTS

Introduction

1. Frederick, Prince of Wales and his sisters by Philippe Mercier, 1733. In the courtyard garden on the north side of the White House, Frederick plays the cello in relative harmony with his sisters: Anne, Princess Royal on the harpsichord and Caroline on the mandolin. Princess Amelia, whose love of gossip often led her to fall out with Frederick, stares out with a book of poems by Milton open on her lap – is she reading Paradise Lost? *In the background can be seen the princesses' house, Kew Palace.*

KEW PALACE is Britain's smallest royal palace and the third building to bear that name. It lies within the Royal Botanic Gardens and has long gone by the affectionate name of 'the Dutch House', reflecting its compact proportions and early seventeenth-century curved gables, which make it one of the most intriguing buildings in the country. Within its walls, almost five hundred years of history lie concealed, but only recently have the full story and the importance of the building become known.

Kew Palace began life as a rich merchant's country house in 1631, resting on the foundations of an earlier courtier's lodge. In 1729, it caught the attention of Queen Caroline, who leased the house to provide accommodation for her daughters. Later, two future British monarchs spent their formative years within its walls, when it was brought into service as their dormitory and school-room. In the wider landscape around the palace, the royal pleasure grounds were gradually cultivated to become an internationally renowned centre for botanical study and a treasury of garden architecture.

George III and his family form the central thread of Kew's story. Most famously, in the winter of 1788–89 George III and his immediate family retreated to Kew as the King suffered his first bout of porphyria, which at the time was diagnosed as madness. During the first years of the nineteenth century, the royal family lodged in the present palace, a most unroyal building that is decidedly domestic in scale and character.

Nevertheless, George III's long reign witnessed the stirrings of the Industrial Revolution, the formation of the British Empire and, some would argue, the foundations of the modern world. Scientific endeavour, the discovery of new lands, agricultural improvement, botany, astronomy and social improvement were focused as though through a lens at Kew. In all this, the King occupies a pivotal place as patron, champion and student. This little palace briefly lay at the epicentre of national and even international affairs. It was at once a place of recuperation for the King, a stifling nunnery for his unmarried daughters and a retreat for Queen Charlotte, who died here in 1818.

Queen Victoria gave the palace to the nation in 1898. Her parents had been married there and she developed a particular attachment and affection for the building. After being open to the public for almost a century, Kew Palace was closed in 1996 for an extensive programme of research, repair and re-presentation. In 2006 it emerged once again to take its rightful place in telling the story of our nation's history.

Note: As the presence of several royal houses at Kew can be confusing, the reader is directed to the map on the inside front cover for clarification. Of the three principal buildings, Richmond Lodge, which developed from a late seventeenth-century royal hunting lodge, lay closest to Richmond, but was unrelated to the medieval palace there. Further north on the Green, Kew Palace was originally the Fortrey mansion and is sometimes called the Dutch House. The nearby White House was originally the Capel mansion, and was later known as Kew House.

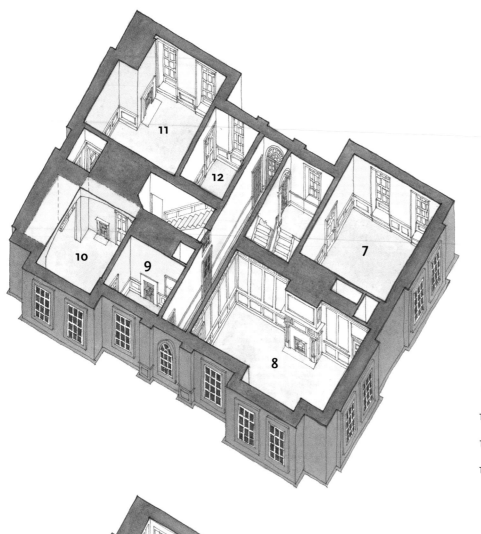

FIRST FLOOR

7 Queen's Boudoir

8 Queen's Drawing Room

9 Princess Elizabeth's Dressing Room

10 Princess Elizabeth's Bedroom

11 Queen Charlotte's Bedroom

12 Queen's Ante-room

LOCATION OF
DEMOLISHED
WEST WING

GROUND FLOOR

1 Ante-room

2 King's Library

3 Pages' Waiting Room

4 King's Dining Room

5 King's Breakfast Room

6 Staircase

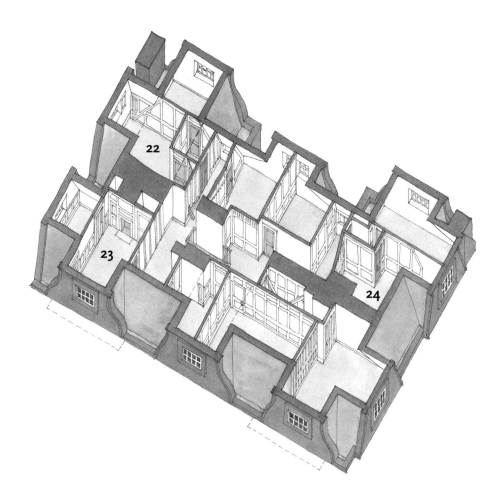

THIRD FLOOR

22, 23, 24 Servants' Bedrooms

Many of the attic rooms were
used for storage or as bedrooms

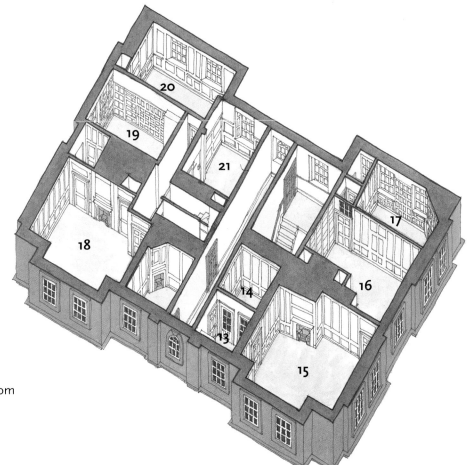

SECOND FLOOR

13 Ante-room

14 Inner Closet 'Powder Room'

15 Princess Augusta's Bedroom

16 Princess Amelia's Bedroom

17 Princess Amelia's Dressing Room

18 Housekeeper's Room

19, 20, 21 The use of these
rooms is not known

The Banks *of the* THAMES: ROYAL Sheen *and* Richmond

Kew becomes a retreat for wealthy courtiers, who build a series of houses close to Richmond Palace. Among them is the Earl of Leicester, who may have constructed the first building on the site of Kew Palace.

2. The Thames at Richmond, with the Old Royal Palace *(detail), c. 1620. The turreted lodgings of Richmond Palace provide a dramatic background to this scene of a group of performers watched by amused onlookers on the banks of the Thames. This painting, by an unknown artist, gives an impression of the pleasant surroundings of Richmond Palace.*

Early development along the River Thames

Royal interest in the margins of the River Thames around Kew extends into the distant past, when this loop of the meandering river was part of the royal estate of Kingston-upon-Thames and its well-watered meadows were considered an important resource.

At the foundation of the English state in the tenth century, when the county of Surrey itself came into being, Kew formed the northern periphery of a large administrative area based on Kingston. This town may be the site of an older royal centre known as 'Freoricsburna', where King Offa of Mercia (757–96) and later West Saxon kings witnessed royal charters and held court. Kew, or Keyho, 'a spur of land', was a remote, outlying part of this great estate. To the south of Kew, another small estate emerged at Sheen, which has been known since the late fifteenth century as Richmond. When the great taxation survey Domesday Book was compiled at the command of William the Conqueror in 1086, neither Kew nor Sheen was separately enumerated, but Kingston was divided into many small manors, deriving value and income from five mills and three fisheries, with forty acres of meadow. Humphrey the Chamberlain was charged with collecting the queen's wool here. Kew and Sheen were undoubtedly a vital component of this rich resource.

The main focus of settlement lay around Kew Green, an area of common pasture grazed by the manor's tenant farmers that formed a broad, funnel-like shape, which developed to corral sheep and cattle from the meadows and waste towards the main road to Kingston. Here they could be despatched to market, secured in pens or used to provide manure. The northernmost tip of Kew Green lay close to the present site of the palace, beyond which thin, narrow strip fields were cultivated in rotation. This was a pattern that remained until gradual enclosure and consolidation in the seventeenth and eighteenth centuries. Ultimately, the key to settlement was the Green, with buildings spread along its edges. A distinct, compact village never existed and a separate parish was not created until 1769.

Royal interest in the area was stimulated from the late thirteenth century by visits from Edward I (1272–1307) in pursuit of good hunting in a warren and park at Sheen. The manor there eventually passed into royal hands and Edward II (1307–27) founded a short-lived Carmelite monastery nearby in 1314. More frequent royal attendance can be traced through visits from the disgraced dowager Queen Isabella, the 'she-wolf' of France who had conspired with her lover Mortimer against her husband, and who was ferried under close confinement between various manors after her downfall. On her death in 1358, the young Edward III (1327–77) began the transformation of the manor house into a palace with a gatehouse, clock tower, courtyards, gardens, vineyards and fishponds. It was to Sheen that the King increasingly retreated for privacy in old age; there he died after suffering a stroke in June 1377. The final act of the reign, played out in his bedchamber at Sheen, was

In 1354 a mob broke into Sheen Palace, assaulted Queen Isabella's men and servants, and stole her "goods as well as hares, conies, partridges and pheasants".

From the earliest days of Sheen Palace, large tracts of the surrounding areas were created as royal parks for the purpose of hunting.

Elizabeth I died at Richmond Palace on 24 March 1603, aged 69. According to her chaplain, she died "mildly like a lamb, easily like a ripe apple from the tree".

3. Anne of Bohemia
(1366–1394) was married to
Richard II in 1382 when both
were only fifteen. On her death
from plague at Sheen, Richard
was said to be "wild with grief",
refusing to enter her apartments
for a year before finally ordering
their demolition. This
contemporary illustration of
her deathbed is from a copy of
The Chronicles of Froissart.

that of his last mistress, Alice Perrers, who tugged the jewelled rings from the fingers of the dying monarch.

Richard II (1377–99) initiated changes that enhanced the luxury and prestige of the site. He built a miniature palace as a summerhouse on an island in the Thames, commissioned 2000 glazed tiles for his bathroom and continued to embellish the palace throughout the 1380s. When his beloved queen, Anne of Bohemia, died of the plague at the palace in 1394 (fig. 3), the grief-stricken Richard ordered the demolition of many buildings. This was unlikely to have been comprehensive as the gardens continued to be maintained, but no further activity was recorded there until the second decade of the fifteenth century.

Henry V (1413–22), perhaps seeking expiation for the sins of his father, Henry IV (1399–1413), in illegally seizing the crown from Richard II, found in Sheen an ideal place both to live and to reinforce the precarious legitimacy of his claim to the throne. He refurbished the derelict palace and founded two great monasteries. The House of Jesus of Bethlehem, established in the park near the site of the present Observatory, was, most unusually, given to the Carthusian Order. The rigorously spiritual monks lived

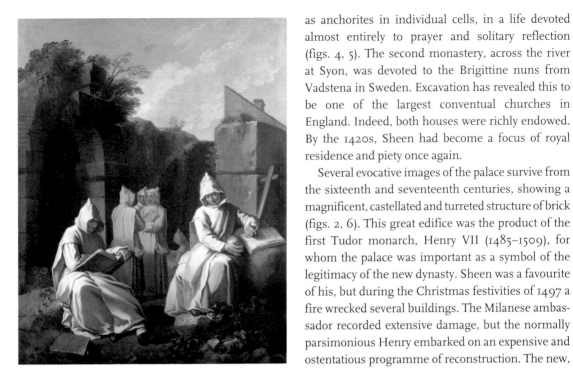

4. *A romantic view of Carthusian monks in meditation by Etienne Jeaurat (1699–1789). The Carthusians were founded in 1084 by St Bruno at Chartreuse near Grenoble in France. Their guiding principle was, and remains, contemplation through solitude, prayer and work.*

as anchorites in individual cells, in a life devoted almost entirely to prayer and solitary reflection (figs. 4, 5). The second monastery, across the river at Syon, was devoted to the Brigittine nuns from Vadstena in Sweden. Excavation has revealed this to be one of the largest conventual churches in England. Indeed, both houses were richly endowed. By the 1420s, Sheen had become a focus of royal residence and piety once again.

Several evocative images of the palace survive from the sixteenth and seventeenth centuries, showing a magnificent, castellated and turreted structure of brick (figs. 2, 6). This great edifice was the product of the first Tudor monarch, Henry VII (1485–1509), for whom the palace was important as a symbol of the legitimacy of the new dynasty. Sheen was a favourite of his, but during the Christmas festivities of 1497 a fire wrecked several buildings. The Milanese ambassador recorded extensive damage, but the normally parsimonious Henry embarked on an expensive and ostentatious programme of reconstruction. The new,

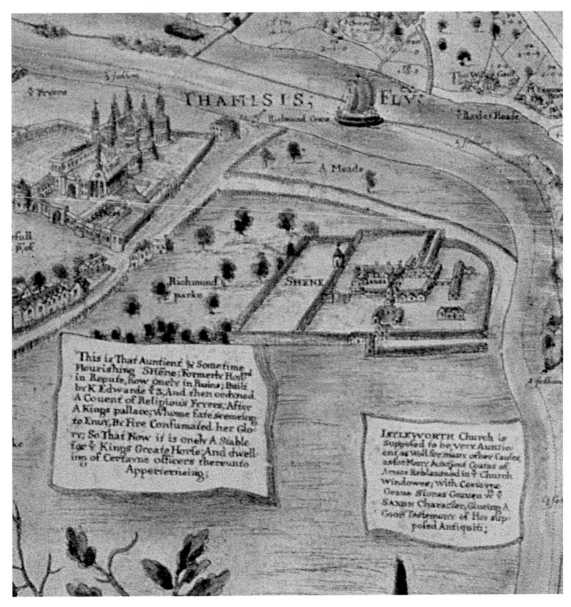

5. *Detail of Moses Glover's map of 1635, showing the dissolved Carthusian monastery at Sheen. The pattern of individual cells clustered round a cloistered garden was still recognizable a century after its downfall. To the left are the towers of Richmond.*

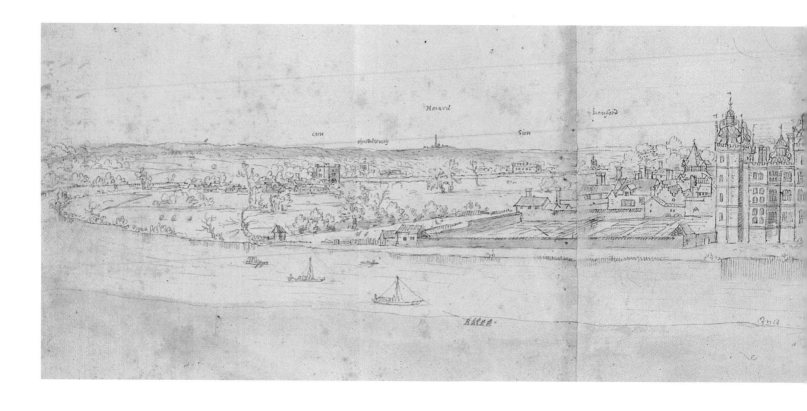

6. *Richmond Palace by Antonis van den Wyngaerde, 1562. The site was dominated by the central lodgings, which formed the main residential accommodation for the royal family. Lying adjacent (right), a long galleried walkway extended from the palace to the tennis courts by way of the Friars' church, enclosing the privy orchard and gardens.*

gorgeously ornate and modern building was rechristened Richmond, in honour of the King's earlier title of Earl of Richmond. The palace was henceforth to be the focus of courtly entertainments, which would increase in splendour during the reign of Henry VIII (1509–47).

Development at Kew

From the beginning of the sixteenth century, Kew was drawn into the orbit of Richmond Palace. Henry VIII's court was populated by wealthy, ambitious and powerful men, and attendance became far more important than hitherto. For the first time, members of the nobility aspired to create their own houses nearby, both to maintain a retreat near the court and to avoid the intrigues that dogged life within the palace. As the immediate area around Richmond was given over to parkland or monastic property, Kew was a natural choice and local landowners such as Thomas Byrkes were quick to capitalize on demands for small plots of land and suitable houses. The earliest mansion or dwelling identified from the records belonged to the Earl of Devon and was in existence by the end of the fifteenth century. In 1508 the Spanish ambassador wrote that Catherine of Aragon, briefly married to Henry VII's eldest son, Prince Arthur, but now widowed, was staying in a "lonely house which is in a park" at Kew, which was probably this house. No physical trace has been found and not even its exact site is known. By the first decades of the sixteenth century, it was joined by houses built by Sir Charles Somerset, later Earl of Worcester, Henry Norris, Henry VIII's Esquire of the Body (who was later implicated in the

supposed adultery of Anne Boleyn and executed), and Sir John Dudley, another aspiring courtier. Properties such as these changed hands frequently and many questions remain about their location and form.

Sir John Dudley (1502?–1553) may represent the first tangible link with the actual site of Kew Palace as the owner of the land on which the palace now stands. An ambitious and influential man, he seized power from Protector Somerset during the minority of Edward VI, was created Duke of Northumberland and rose to become the most powerful man in England. He sealed his fate with the attempt to place Lady Jane Grey on the throne in 1553 in the place of Edward's sister Mary. After his execution, his lands at Kew were forfeit, but within a few years a new generation in the person of his son Robert Dudley (fig. 7) was to regain these lands from the hands of a new and adoring sovereign, Elizabeth I (1558–1603).

The first house to be built on the site of Kew Palace was a relatively modest Tudor structure, most likely of brick. Evidence for it survives in abundance in the undercroft of the palace (fig. 8). Here, two brick-built vaulted chambers can be dated stylistically to the mid-sixteenth century. A vaulted passage leads to the east from the main chambers, where a well survives beneath its own domed brick cover. The undercroft does not extend beneath the entire palace, suggesting that the earlier house was smaller and possibly orientated differently, facing west, instead of south as it does now, with a service wing to the rear. The date of the vault and the tortuously complex sequence of land transfers that traces ownership in the area indicate that a good candidate for the building of this

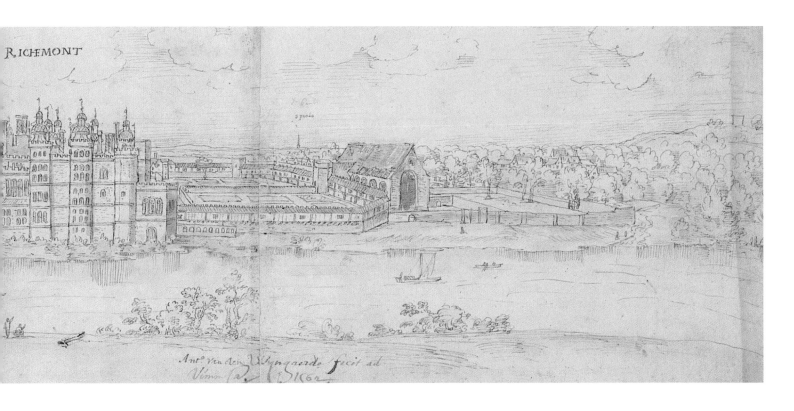

RICHEMONT

Ant° van der Wÿngaerde fecit ad
Vivm [?] 1562

7. Robert Dudley, Earl of
Leicester *(1532–1588)*
attributed to Steven van der
Muelen, c. 1560–65. Dudley
was the fifth son of John, Duke
of Northumberland. He rose to
be favourite of Queen Elizabeth,
using his charm and good looks
to win influence, power and
land. His ultimate ambition
to marry her was, however,
thwarted by the Queen's shrewd
understanding of his intentions.

8. *The undercroft at Kew*
Palace, c. 1935. The ribs
of the pointed arches spring
from fat, octagonal shafts
that belong to the earlier,
mid-sixteenth-century house.
In the 1960s the plaster render
seen in this photograph was
removed to reveal a structure
entirely of brick.

Little may be said with certainty of this earlier house, though perhaps it had something of the appearance of lodgings or the type of ancillary accommodation that survives adjacent to larger houses elsewhere. At Chenies Manor in Buckinghamshire, the sixteenth-century mansion was augmented by Sir John Russell with lodgings for the reception of Elizabeth I and her courtiers, and included a small but richly decorated building in the garden (fig. 10). This survived as a partially collapsed ruin until recent refurbishment; like Kew, there is an undercroft of similar size, above which were large single chambers at ground- and first-floor levels, with little garderobes and an impressive stair turret providing access. This forms an important comparison, because size was not the first consideration for courtly convenience. Instead, the visual status of the building, its brick, crow-stepped gables, large windows and an imposing staircase were deemed more appropriate for a high courtier. At Kew the quality of the undercroft, with its Flemish tiled floor, attests a similar status. Out-houses and barns, which existed in the early seventeenth century, would have accommodated the needs of a wealthy noble household such as Dudley's. Moreover, the size of the building would have been no barrier to an intimate dinner with the Queen.

10. *Chenies Manor, Buckinghamshire. This small garden building was embellished for "the quietness of my Lord Cecil", Elizabeth I's elderly chief minister, as a retreat from the turmoil of court. In both scale and use it resembles the earlier lodge that existed on the site of Kew Palace.*

house was Robert Dudley himself. His family lands were restored to him in 1558 and the undercroft, built around this time, is of no mean house but a high-status, if small, residence. Excavations of the site of a neighbouring mansion known as the White House, just a few metres to the south, have revealed traces of a Tudor basement there, but this is likely to have been the house of the Awberry family, who were broadly contemporary. The identification of Dudley as the builder of this precursor to the palace must remain a cautious one, but it is important because Elizabeth I was entertained in his house at Kew in 1563, where she was fed and entertained in expensive style. The accounts record that the Queen was offered pineapples, then a highly exotic and rare fruit.

The death of Elizabeth I in 1603 marked the beginning of a slow decline in the fortunes of Richmond Palace, which culminated in the sale of the buildings under the Commonwealth. Though the deer park was enlarged under Charles I (1625–49), the aristocratic taste for Kew waned, leaving many of the houses to pass by sale into the hands of merchants – a new and rising class emerging in the City of London.

11. *Christopher Saxton produced a series of maps for his pioneering atlas of 1579. They reflect not only an interest in cartography but also improved techniques of surveying and engraving in the Elizabethan period. The map of Surrey shows how rural the area around Kew was.*

OPPOSITE 9. *Henry, Prince of Wales by Robert Peake the Elder, c. 1610. The Prince had ambitious plans to revitalize Richmond Palace, but these were curtailed by his untimely death in 1612. His riverside gardens at Richmond can be glimpsed through the window.*

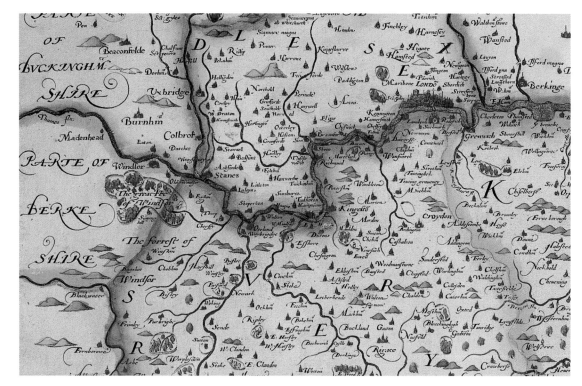

KEW, *the* Playground *of Merchant* PRINCES 1620–1720

Kew becomes established as a sought-after residential area for the court. It is put firmly on the map when the Prince and Princess of Wales take Richmond Lodge as their country house in 1718.

12. A view of Richmond Lodge from the south, from John Lawrence's A New System of Agriculture, *1726. The Great Avenue from the lodge to the river was planted by George London for William III. The avenue of chestnut trees in the foreground leading to Richmond Green may have been planted at the same time.*

The beginnings of renewed interest

Three houses define a renewal of interest in Kew. Richmond Lodge lay just to the south of the boundary of the present-day Botanic Gardens, while to the north, at what used to form the tapering end of the ancient common known as Kew Green, lay two houses in close proximity: the Capel mansion (later known as the White House) and the Fortrey mansion. Both houses would be taken over in the early eighteenth century in the course of royal expansion. The latter house survives today as Kew Palace.

Though aristocratic interest at Kew had dwindled, new money was poised to take over the leases of the houses and lodges that peppered the area. Despite rising tensions between King and Parliament in the years before the English Civil War, London was enjoying burgeoning economic prosperity. Its streets were populated by entrepreneurial merchants importing luxuries and raw materials, by ennobled civil servants, diplomats and refugees from Catholic Europe. At the apex of this system, Charles I presided over a cultured coterie of courtiers, whose patronage of the arts and architecture played an important rôle as a vehicle for progress and an expression of royal power. The Italian-inspired Neo-classicism imported by Inigo Jones and his followers, and displayed at the Banqueting House in Whitehall, was startling to English eyes. A new class of men emerging in the livery companies and markets was eager to express its wealth, and the style soon percolated through the various social strata, suitably adapted and simplified,

to appear on buildings all over the capital. Dudley Digges, Member of Parliament and Virginia Adventurer, noted that "The City of London is a place that seeks only to enrich themselves, and then away they go to the country into the second descent." He described the country houses or villas that proliferated as a place where this second generation of moneyed men could act out the life of a country squire, away from the unwholesome City, with none of the inconveniences of managing vast estates, extensive travel or the onerous maintenance of a large household. These men were drawn from a variety of backgrounds.

Samuel Fortrey, 1567–1643

The arrival in late Elizabethan England of Protestants fleeing persecution from France and the Spanish Netherlands was not universally welcomed. However, like the later Huguenots, they found a niche, brought with them new and valuable skills, and integrated quickly into the fabric of English society. Around 1567, one such family travelled from France or Flanders to find a haven in London. Nicholas and Margaret de la Forterie arrived with their five children and set up house near the Tower of London. Nicholas was a merchant and, like his compatriots, was treated at times with suspicion by the authorities. His sons John and Samuel followed their father into business, though it is not known in what commodities they dealt. John was part of a group known as the Entercourse of Merchant Strangers, which dealt in the

The poet Alexander Pope, with Jonathan Swift, the novelist and essayist, and John Gay, the playwright, were described by the pardoned Jacobite Viscount Bolingbroke as "the three yahoos of Twickenham".

Tartlets.

Queen Caroline built four houses on Richmond Green to accommodate her Maids of Honour. A local baker created Maids of Honour tarts as a compliment to them.

Dr Alured Clarke, who introduced Stephen Duck to Queen Caroline, described "the thresher with all his defects a superior genius to Mr Pope". Jonathan Swift rated his poetry "not worth a straw".

TOP 13. *The cut and rubbed brick cartouche over the entrance to Kew Palace, which entwines the initials of Samuel and Catherine Fortrey. As the couple already had a young family by 1631, this panel and the accompanying date-stones are likely to commemorate the raising of the house rather than their marriage.*

TOP RIGHT 14. *An example of rubbed brick at Kew Palace. The brick mason rendered all the moulding, window surrounds, horizontal banding and Classical motifs that would normally be expressed in stone, plaster or timber by cutting and rubbing soft bricks.*

ABOVE 15. *Boston Manor, Brentford. Lady Mary Reade's country villa has tripartite gables of brick, but with their own idiosyncrasies. Like Kew, the house is now much altered, but important early elements such as the staircase and several decorated ceilings survive.*

import and export of all manner of things. Samuel, from his will, is known to have part-owned a ship, the *Pearcey*. Like many merchants, however, he remains an enigma apart from the basic outline of his life, and no image of him survives. He married Catherine de Latfeur and with her had several children. By middle age he had become sufficiently wealthy to look around for a suitable country house and from 1619 rented the old Tudor lodge at Kew – possibly Robert Dudley's house. A large parcel of land had been purchased some thirty years previously by Sir John Portman (died 1612), a Somerset landowner, and the lodge may have survived with a second building nearby that came to be known as the Dairy House. By 1620, Samuel Fortrey was already a tenant but Sir John's widow and her second husband, Edward Popham, leased the property to him in his brother's name in July 1620 for nine years at £17 per annum. When this term expired, he took a more secure lease on the property and embarked on the construction of the enduring monument to the period at royal Kew.

The Fortrey mansion

The date and authorship of the Fortrey mansion, now known as Kew Palace, survive in a cut brick cartouche over the door, which proclaims the year 1631 (fig. 13). There are no building accounts and, as in the case of many such houses, a lack of documentation has sparked wide discussion of the varied influences on houses of this period and type. What was built at Kew is, to modern eyes, a curious hybrid of style and proportion, but this is just one example of a type that varied greatly in style, sharing only general characteristics. Barely a handful of these early villas now survive in London, so that they seem exotic and strangely out of place in the organic line of architectural progress. Often they were embellished with all manner of borrowed motifs, drawn both from the architect's pattern book and from the repertoire of the master bricklayers and masons who constructed them, who drew in turn on the traditions of timber-framing. The result is a freer individuality and expression, known as Artisan Mannerism, which can be seen at nearby Boston Manor in Brentford (fig. 15), or at Forty Hall at Enfield, built for the haber-dasher Sir Nicholas Rainton in 1629–35. Samuel Fortrey's mansion, however, continues to stand as an epitome of the period: novel and precocious.

In its day, it would have appeared conspicuously expensive. An unknown mason raised the new build-ing on the cellars of the old lodge, enlarging and reorientating the new house. From brick he crafted a jewel box, with windows on all sides admitting light through tall transomed and mullioned casements, at the same time embellishing and borrowing indis-criminately from a wide palette of motifs. The brick bondwork, known from the seventeenth century as Flemish bond, needed skill and precision, but most importantly it was visibly expensive and new (fig. 14). The degree of fine craftsmanship required to create the intricate window embrasures and curves must have been costly. Crowning all four façades is the most recognizable aspect of the building, which has given it a distinctive identity: the shaped and curved gables, with alternating triangular and arched pedi-ments pierced by little attic dormer windows with

their own rustication. Above all, its architectural unity was provided by an ochre colourwash. This tra-ditional application used earth pigments mixed with animal glue or lime and has recently been reinstated.

The building has been known as 'the Dutch House' or 'the Red House' since the nineteenth century. The unusual block-massing, the early form of bondwork, Fortrey's origins and, above all, these gables have created a confused mythology about the mansion, that it is somehow a Dutch building transported to England. However, it was nothing more than the product of a cosmopolitan city and, had more such houses survived, it might instead be recognized as a London regional style. Its influences are inevitably foreign, but mostly secondhand, with strong paral-lels elsewhere in England. Blickling Hall in Norfolk has a service wing contemporary with Kew that has both shaped gables and Flemish bondwork. Closer to hand, so-called 'Dutch' gables also survive at Rawdon House in Hoddesdon (Hertfordshire), built for Sir Marmaduke Rawdon, a wealthy merchant, in 1622. Indeed, the shaped gable has few affinities with Holland at this time, showing closer parallels with examples on English homes of the late Elizabethan and Jacobean period, including some nearby such as Fairfax House, Putney (fig. 16).

Fortrey's building was equally sumptuous inside

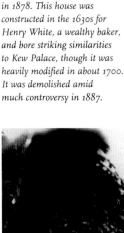

16. Fairfax House, Putney, in 1878. This house was constructed in the 1630s for Henry White, a wealthy baker, and bore striking similarities to Kew Palace, though it was heavily modified in about 1700. It was demolished amid much controversy in 1887.

17. *The plaster overdoor decoration in the King's Dining Room is finely executed with a moustachioed imperial bust, shell-niche, jewelled bosses and little sockets for candles or ornaments.*

BELOW 18. *The King's Dining Room. This room was originally the hall of the Jacobean mansion. Both here and in the King's Library, bulky sculpted chimney pieces of limestone were inserted into older surrounds. Stylistically they appear closely related to works by William Kent and may represent his hand in the modernization of the house from 1730.*

and the fragments that survive suggest that it was extravagantly decorated. Originally the central corridor from the door formed an open passage with the great hall to the right. Within the hall, now called the King's Dining Room, an overmantel with the characteristic Jacobean decorative ornament known as strapwork survives (fig. 18). The door into the parlour beyond (the King's Breakfast Room) preserves magnificent moulded plasterwork (fig. 17). Most rooms were panelled in oak, which was in turn painted and decorated. On the opposite side of the house, the room now called the King's Library was probably a common parlour and preserves some of its original panelling and elaborate Jacobean decoration over the fireplace (fig. 19). Here, one of the most important decorative schemes in the house was uncovered during investigations in 2005. Several schemes were painted directly on the panelling during the seventeenth century, including a theatrical graining of brown and yellow ochre, with an overmantel later decorated with a figurative scheme in grey, white and black, clearly intended to capture the appearance of marble and carving. The more sumptuous rooms lay

on the eastern side of the house, but here on the west side, a room of lesser status, possibly even adjoining a kitchen, preserves costly decorations of great skill.

The existing staircase is a splendid example of about 1730 (fig. 20), but the original would have been an important and ostentatious sign of wealth, rising like a great tower through the house into the attics, and painted with a *trompe-l'œil* scheme replicating its balusters on the flanking walls. Fragments of this survive on the final, attic landing; they lay hidden behind lime paint and an eighteenth-century skirting until 1988 and were noticed only in 2005. They show thick, squared newels, piled up with decorative finials, and fat, turned balusters to a heavily moulded handrail (fig. 21).

The first floor was the most important, containing the Great Chamber or Dining Room, a music room and principal bedchambers. The south-facing room, which is now known as the Queen's Drawing Room (fig. 22), retains a frieze of strapwork and Classical motifs, and a chimney piece of great magnificence. It is inconceivable that this room did not have an elaborate plaster ceiling, such as still exists in the

19. The King's Library, c. 1950. The central panels of the overmantel are flanked by arched niches that have 'green men' as their keystones. The panels were painted with a grey, white and black figurative scheme embellished with gilding, which was rediscovered in 2005.

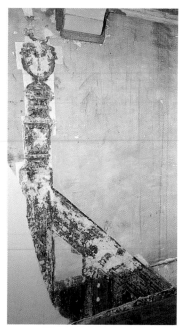

ABOVE 21. *In the seventeenth century, the palace was provided with an elaborate open-well staircase, which rose into the roof. Fragments of a wall painting that would have mimicked its form were found in the attic in 2005. Conservation revealed elaborate newels over two metres in height, painted in subtle tones with gilding. In the 1670s it was modified to appear even more expensive, with piled up and elaborately carved finials, and tapering, vase-like balusters beneath a heavily moulded handrail, all repainted to look like stone.*

20. *The main staircase at Kew Palace is one of two built in the early 1730s as part of the modernization of the palace. The other is a slightly more modest housekeeper's or back stair. The main stair has delicate turned balusters, scrolled brackets and a rounded curtail at the base, typical of a kind found in wealthier houses in both town and country.*

22. *The Queen's Drawing Room. Several features survive from 1631, including the delicate strapwork frieze, which extends around the top of the walls. The heavy panelling below was probably fitted in the 1690s.*

23. *The Great Chamber at Boston Manor, Brentford, built for Lady Mary Reade in 1629. The ceiling is a virtuoso example of the plasterer's art, encrusted in high relief with playful imagery and scenes of mythology. Similarly ostentatious decoration must also have existed at Kew.*

24. *The ceiling of the Queen's Boudoir. The only surviving seventeenth-century decorated ceiling at Kew Palace has a geometric lattice of narrow ribs, which frame hand-moulded medallions. These depict the five senses. The sense of hearing lies at the centre, suggesting that the room was originally used for music or entertainment.*

Great Chamber of Boston Manor (fig. 23). Fortrey's own will gives us our single documentary insight into the decoration, when he bequeathed a number of gilt leather hangings from this room to his son.

Kew Palace may have been adorned with many decorated plaster ceilings but only a single example remains, in the Queen's Boudoir (fig. 24). At second-floor level, several rooms retain a wide array of panelling types of the seventeenth century, and two doors from lesser bedrooms or closets survive in their original position. These were originally grained to appear like oak in an attempt to give the house a more luxurious appearance.

Only a few metres away from the palace stood a second mansion, an enigmatic house that had been sold at the same time as the Fortrey mansion, to Sir Richard Bennett, and which had been inherited by his daughter Dorothy, Lady Capel. Almost nothing is known of this house, which was later to be redeveloped as a royal residence known as the White House, but archaeological evidence suggests that it was of Tudor origin. The diarist John Evelyn visited it several times, observing that it was old, and of

timber, but had the finest gardens with the choicest fruit. On a later visit, he described the hall "with a kind of cupola, and in a niche was an artificial fountain". There were greenhouses for oranges and myrtles, and possibly a rustic cupola made with poles. Fortrey's house may likewise have been surrounded with carefully cultivated grounds, although its seventeenth-century-style gardens are entirely modern creations (fig. 165).

The later history

No long-standing emotional attachment was ever forged between Samuel's mansion and the Fortrey family. Many such rural mansions fell by the wayside as fortunes waxed and waned or families decanted to more exalted estates. Gradually the family was drawn away. By the time Samuel died in 1643, the house had already been assigned to his son Samuel junior, who departed for greater challenges in draining the rural fenlands of the Isle of Ely and leased the property. It is difficult to know whether the family ever lived in it for much of the latter half of the seventeenth century, and only through the various leasing agreements is it known that they still held a vested interest. However, there were always merchants who chose to recycle old houses rather than build anew, and Sir Richard Levett, tobacco merchant and later Lord Mayor of London, was one such (fig. 25). He purchased the lease of the house in 1697, drawn, no doubt, by the good qualities of Kew and the desirability of a country retreat. As his tenure on the house was brief, modifications to the house were few. He probably modernized the Great Chamber with heavy and expensive bolection-moulded panelling, which remains, but otherwise little is known.

Levett died in 1710 and the old Fortrey house was inherited by his daughter Mary. Meanwhile, its close neighbour, Lady Capel's house, had been inherited in 1721 by her great-niece Elizabeth, who was married to Lord Molyneux, an intimate of George II and Queen Caroline. Events a few years later were to precipitate the transfer of both mansions into the hands of the royal family, but by the late 1720s it seems that both ladies were keen to dispose of their respective inheritances.

Richmond Lodge, 1619–1727
First residents

To the south of the present-day Royal Botanic Gardens, Richmond Lodge had emerged through a slightly different sequence of events. It was situated less than half a mile from Richmond Palace; the surrounding parkland had been Crown property until the advent of the Commonwealth. It stood close to the site of the dissolved Carthusian monastery, which by the early eighteenth century provided the location for the hamlet of West Sheen, with its enclave of sought-after villas and views across the river to the great house of Syon. In 1619, James I (1603–25) had Robert Stickles, Clerk of the Works, build him a hunting lodge with a new hunting ground of 370 acres. This is possibly the first mention of the house that would become known as Richmond Lodge. The Parliamentary survey of Richmond Palace of 1649 recorded "a fair gate of good ornament to the House, standing towards the park". In the sale of all Crown property following the execution of Charles I, the park adjoining Richmond Green was purchased by a Mr William Brome, who let the lodge, advertised as "a very pleasant seat and habitation for a private gentleman", to Sir Thomas Jervoise. By 1667, it had been let to Captain Richard Brett and his wife Catherine, the daughter of Roger Boyle, 1st Earl of Orrery. Many acres of the estate were then parcelled up and let to several tenants. Though the grounds now consisted of little more than a length of land and a strip of woodland with access westward to the river bank, there remained good hunting and any short-comings did not deter the lodge's next tenant – William III (1689–1702).

King William was "so well pleased with the situa-

26. James Butler, 2nd Duke of Ormonde *by or after Michael Dahl, 1714. "A perfect Trianon, everything in it and about it answerable to the grandeur and magnificence of its great master" was a contemporary description of Ormonde's estate at Richmond. The Duke became involved in the Jacobite Rebellion of 1715, which sought to overthrow the Hanoverians and bring the Catholic son of James II to the British throne. As a consequence his estates were forfeit and he fled to France.*

tion of the house in the park where he lay" that he purchased the estate and "gave orders for some additional apartments and enlarging of the gardens". From 1693 to 1695 building work costing some £3500 took place under the supervision of Henry Simmonds, the Clerk of the Works for Hampton Court, while the famous royal gardener George London was employed for "making and levelling the great Walke leading from the house to the Thames, planting it with trees" (fig. 12). One of William III's neighbours at Richmond was Sir William Temple, a diplomatic envoy to The Netherlands and a close associate of the King. Like William he was a keen gardener and famously grew excellent nectarines in his West Sheen garden, where reportedly the King demonstrated the Dutch method of cutting asparagus for the edification of Temple's secretary, the young Jonathan Swift.

Although the house was never intended for any purpose other than as a hunting lodge, William furnished the interior extravagantly. The King's bedchamber was provided with a new velvet bed with silk fringe and matching hangings, chairs, stools and screen, with an antechamber curtained with white fringed damask. At the head of the stairs a chamber was prepared for the Earl of Portland and over the King's bedchamber was a panelled room, "where it is supposed Mr Cappell will lye". Sir Henry Capel owned the large estate to the north at Kew and was Steward of the Manor of Richmond. He was to lie in great state, his allocated bedchamber and dressing room hung with crimson and gold damask. It is doubtful whether he ever enjoyed this privilege, for he died the following year, in 1696.

In the spring of 1694, William III accorded a lease on his new property, both house and park, to John Latten, his equerry and close friend, for a peppercorn rent, "as a mark of favour and for his encouragement to improve the premises and to preserve the game there for his Majesty's disport". It is probable that William had little inclination for hunting from this time. His consort, Queen Mary II, died of smallpox at the age of thirty-two in the final days of 1694, and grief and wars took him to Europe for much of the second half of that decade.

Shortly after William III's death in 1702, Latten, who owned a larger estate in Esher, sold off his share in the lease at Richmond to James Butler, 2nd Duke of Ormonde (fig. 26). Although newly appointed Lord Lieutenant of Ireland, Ormonde spent his summer months in England. He took great interest in the property at Richmond, employing the Earl of Ranelagh to supervise a rebuilding and enlargement of the south front of the lodge. Early in 1705, Ormonde was notified that, as he had requested, £50 had been paid to Vanbrugh, that the necessary demolition had been completed and the painting almost

OPPOSITE 27. *Detail from a painting of Syon House by Jan Griffier the Elder, c. 1710, showing the north face of Richmond Lodge with its new west wing. This view largely corresponds to John Rocque's elevation drawing (fig. 42), showing a relatively modest villa of brick in typical seventeenth-century style. In the foreground the terrace, summerhouse and canal can be seen with the hamlet of West Sheen in the background.*

28. George II as Prince of Wales with his wife Princess Caroline and his father, George I. George I inherited the throne from Queen Anne, his third cousin, in 1714. He was fifty-four when he acceded and was divorced. Instead of a queen, he brought two unattractive mistresses to England, as well as his son and daughter-in-law. George I spoke very little English and spent much of his time in his native Hanover.

finished and finally that the Duke's furniture would be installed within the month. The estate was enlarged to the north and Ormonde's brother, the Earl of Arran, wrote informing him that he would find as good sport at Richmond as he was then enjoying at Kilkenny. Visiting the area in 1714, Ralph Thoresby recorded in his diary, "the Duke of Ormonde's seat was particularly charming; the house, gardens, avenues, with the park and river adjoining" (fig. 27). The Duke lived in great style at Richmond until his implication in the 1715 Jacobite Rebellion and subsequent exile.

The occupation of Richmond Lodge by the Prince and Princess of Wales

The sequestered house soon fell under the eye of George, Prince of Wales and his wife, Caroline of Ansbach (fig. 28). The spark for the decision by the young couple to make a residence by the River Thames on the Richmond–Kew borders was almost certainly fired by events that took place a few miles upstream in 1716. George I being absent in his native Hanover, the Prince and Princess of Wales hosted a scintillating summer court at Hampton Court Palace. Its success induced a simmering resentment in the King, which erupted into full-blown fury at the christening of the couple's son George in the autumn of the following year. The Prince of Wales was banned from the royal palaces and the King took control of his three daughters, Anne, aged seven,

Amelia, five, and Caroline, three, along with the baby, George, who unsurprisingly failed to thrive and died early the following year at Kensington Palace.

With no royal palace at their disposal the Prince and Princess of Wales were forced to look for alternative accommodation. They took a town house in Leicester Square but still lacked the summer residence their status demanded. The choice of Richmond Lodge was a good one, possibly prompted by several factors. As it was only eight miles from London access was easy, especially by river, yet the area was rural with good hunting in nearby Richmond Park. Richmond itself boasted several centuries of royal occupancy and latterly the surrounding area had become a fashionable resort for many of the set who made up the court of the Prince of Wales. The lodge was sold to the Prince through the Commission and Trustees for Forfeited Estates, and a sale price of £6000 was agreed and settled in July 1719. The Prince also purchased the lavish contents of the entire house and its offices for a mere £709. 1s. 2d.

A detailed inventory of the contents of Richmond Lodge after Ormonde's flight records a dining room with seven double-branched oval glass sconces and a large Delft flowerpot in the fireplace; a bedchamber with yellow damask bed, complete with hangings, matching curtains, easy chairs and six stools with an *en-suite* dressing room and closet; and an area at the top of the stairs set out with card tables and cane chairs (fig. 29). There were bedrooms prepared for

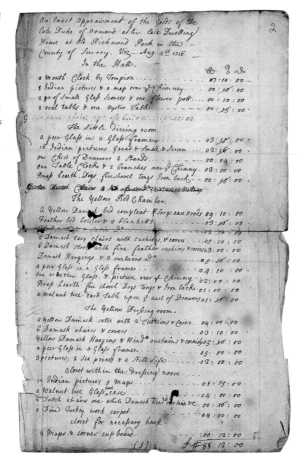

29. An inventory for Richmond Lodge made in August 1717 after the flight of the Duke of Ormonde gives full details of the lavish furnishings that the Prince of Wales acquired when he purchased the house. They included a long-case clock made by Thomas Tompion, the King's clockmaker, and costly damask and silks in the bedchambers.

ladies, a housekeeper, a cook and maids, as well as a lumber room and a nursery. The kitchen was entirely fitted out as were the stables, still-room, laundry, brew-houses and dairy house. Because of the haste and manner of departure of the former tenant, nothing had been removed or sold, down to the "two very ordinary horses, 6 cows, 8 hoggs and poultry" in the yard and an "engine with pipes and coke to fling up ye water for the use of the house". In the barn, £20-worth of peas, rye and wheat lay stored – the likely source of the infestation of rats, requiring the services of a Dorset rat-catcher, who delivered 500 live specimens flushed out of the lodge for Princess Caroline's personal inspection.

The garden contained numerous exotics: a hundred orange trees, as well as pomegranates, nut trees, myrtles and bay trees in tubs and, in addition, eighteen gilded lead urns. The summerhouse was furnished with leather chairs and sofas, and glass sconces, with Dutch seascapes on the walls, and the coach house was complete with coach and four-wheeled chaise. This must have suited the Prince of Wales perfectly, for George I had refused the Prince leave to remove furniture from his former royal apartments. And so the exiled Duke's fully furnished house became the Prince's new summer residence.

The Waleses visited Richmond Lodge every summer from 1718 until 1727, except in 1721 when the birth of their son Prince William at Leicester

House delayed their summer visit until August. Accommodation was always in short supply for royal retainers who, during their attendance at Richmond, were paid 'lodging money' for whatever shelter they could find. Queen Caroline was forced to build a terrace of four houses on Richmond Green to supply her own household's accommodation requirements, and even John, Lord Hervey, her Vice-Chamberlain and intimate confidant, looked forward to when the court moved to Hampton Court "so that I shall no longer be obliged to lead the disagreeable stage-coachman's life which I have done during their stay at Richmond". In addition to costly accommodation, courtiers' finances were further drained by the nightly card parties at the lodge. Henrietta Howard, Countess of Suffolk, the Prince's mistress, perhaps escaped rather lightly, losing only £100 during the first weeks of her stay at Richmond.

An idyllic landscape

The main attraction of Richmond Lodge lay in its situation on the river and in its location. Large houses and estates dotted the banks of the Thames, most notably Ham House but a mile upstream and Syon House, the seat of the Duke of Northumberland, just across the river. Nearby, Twickenham was beginning its own trajectory as "a village remarkable for its abundance of curious seats", which accelerated with reports of a new royal summer residence in the area. Alexander Pope moved to Twickenham in 1718, employing James Gibbs for the design of his Palladian villa. James Johnston, the owner of nearby Orleans House, also commissioned Gibbs to design an octagonal summer-house with the express intention of entertaining the Princess of Wales there. Sir Edward and Lady Mary Wortley Montagu took a neighbouring house and Henrietta Howard came to Twickenham in 1723 when, retiring as the Prince's mistress, she built a Palladian villa by the River Thames at Marble Hill.

Daniel Defoe, writing in the early 1720s, spoke of Richmond in terms of a boom town: "This town and the country adjacent encrease daily in buildings, many noble houses for the accommodation of such, being lately rais'd and more in prospect: but 'tis fear'd should the prince come, for any cause that may happen, to quit that side of the country, those numerous buildings must abate in the value which is now set upon them." Contemporaries spoke of the area as the Frascati of England, the rural Ranelagh – the new focus of fashionable country living and gardening style.

Along with the courtiers came the suppliers and entrepreneurs. Following the arrival of royalty, the spa waters of Richmond Wells, situated on Richmond Hill, were suddenly discovered to be of more benefit to more ailments than had ever previously been supposed, necessitating the building of a pump

come home in the heat of the day with a fever, and (what is worse a hundred times), with a red mark on the forehead from an uneasy hat.

The Princess usually watched the hunt from the sidelines, in the safety of a chaise. There were also *fêtes galantes* and races, one "run under the terrace wall for their royal highnesses to see it. There was an infinite number of people to see them all along the banks; and the river full of boats with people of fashion... . They all stayed until it was late, upon the water to hear the Prince's music, which sounded much sweeter than from the shore."

The gardens at Richmond

"The gardens are very spacious and well kept. There is a fine terrace towards the river. But above all the woods cut out into walks with plenty of birds singing in it make it a most delicious habitation", wrote John Macky in his *Journey through England* (1714) just before the Prince and Princess of Wales took over Richmond Lodge.

30. A prospect of Richmond Lodge from the south by Chatelain after Marco Ricci, c. 1740. Richmond Lodge with its royal occupants and semi-public grounds was a magnet for polite society, who would travel by carriage to promenade in its gardens. The lodge is seen here at the end of its long approach, with well-heeled gentry socializing and 'being seen'.

room and assembly room with ornamental gardens that attracted great numbers of day visitors. A theatre was opened. The *Daily Post* of 23 August 1721 recorded one of a number of royal visits: "On Monday night last Mr Penkethman had the honour to divert their Royal Highnesses, the Prince and Princess of Wales, at his theatre at Richmond, with entertainments of acting and tumbling, performed to admiration; likewise with his picture of the Royal Family down from the King of Bohemia to the young princesses, in which is seen the Nine Muses playing on their several instruments in honour of that august family."

Hunting, however, was still the main attraction of summer country life – a sport also attended by many of the ladies of the court. Alexander Pope, no hunter himself, summed up the ladies' predicament:

Part of the attraction of Richmond for Princess Caroline undoubtedly lay in her passion for gardens. This had developed from her adolescent years spent at Charlottenburg, near Berlin, and, following her marriage, from her time at the Electoral Palace at Herrenhausen in Hanover. Both palaces had magnificent gardens, laid out in a formal manner, as first introduced in France by the celebrated garden designer André Le Nôtre, with long avenues of lime trees, orangeries, terraces, fountains, statues and hornbeam mazes, surrounded by extensive hunting parks. Yet this form of gardening was becoming unfashionable. In her own gardens at Richmond, the Princess of Wales was to experience the thrill of being at the cutting edge of a new style of garden design. As early as September 1719, she consulted Alexander Pope. He introduced her both to Charles Bridgeman, who was at work on Pope's own gardens, and to the new ideas, which were crystallizing into what would become the English landscape garden: "the living landscape chastened and polished, not transformed".

31. The Thames at Twickenham by Peter Tillemans, c. 1724. This view of the river front at Twickenham, seen from the Kew bank, shows a number of substantial villas already in existence by 1724. Alexander Pope's house (centre) is flanked by Lord Radnor's house to the left and the Countess of Ferrers's domed summerhouse to the right.

We all agreed that the life of a maid of honour was of all things the most miserable, and wished that every woman who envied it had a specimen of it. To eat Westphalia ham in a morning, ride over hedges and ditches on borrowed hacks,

ROYALS *in* Residence 1720–30

As Queen Caroline expands her estate from Richmond to Kew, the now vacant 'Dutch House' provides useful overflow accommodation for the elder princesses. For the first time we catch a glimpse through the doorway of this enigmatic house.

32. Queen Caroline of Ansbach with the Duke of Cumberland *by an unknown artist, c. 1730. This painting hangs in the Octagon Room of Orleans House, Twickenham, where Queen Caroline and her children came to dine in August 1729. After separation from her eldest son, Frederick, who had been left in Hanover at George I's insistence, and later from her three older daughters, who were kept under his control, William, Duke of Cumberland, became the Queen's favourite child.*

33. William Kent (1685–1748) *by Bartholomew Dandridge, c. 1730. Kent was a versatile artist, who was known affectionately as "Il Kentino" or "the little rogue". Close friendships formed with noblemen during an extensive stay in Rome (1709–19) won him many commissions as a painter, architect and gardener during later years.*

A family reunited

George I died at Osnabrück in Hanover on 11 June 1727. News of his death was carried to an incredulous new King at Richmond by Robert Walpole, the first minister, three days later.

The royal family was in a state of personal disarray when George II and Queen Caroline came to the throne. Their eldest son, Frederick, who had been left in Hanover at the age of seven on the accession of George I, was now twenty years old and a stranger to both his parents and his siblings. His three older sisters had also been forcibly separated from their parents. Anne, made Princess Royal, was now eighteen, Princess Amelia, commonly called Emily, sixteen and Princess Caroline, fourteen. They had had little opportunity to form any relationship with their younger siblings, William, aged seven, Mary, four, and Louisa, three, nor, of course, with their elder brother.

With the family now reunited around the new King and Queen, Richmond Lodge was clearly too small for the whole brood. William Kent, the architect and landscape designer (fig. 33), was commissioned to produce plans for a grand new palace at Richmond, and, although wooden models show that the proposal was serious, nothing was built (fig. 34). Caroline neatly solved the problem by taking out leases on several houses to the north of her Richmond estate. She acquired a house from the widow of Sir Charles Eyre, who had died early in 1729. This house, it would appear, was initially

intended for Caroline's second surviving and favourite son, William, Duke of Cumberland (fig. 32), but there is no further evidence for his having used it and it later became known as the Queen's House (fig. 50). This enigmatic building, with its flower and kitchen gardens and small wilderness, lay just to the west of Kew Palace. There are several allusions to the Queen's breakfasting at Kew and picking fruit from her gardens there but it is

George Frederick Handel was disinclined to teach music, but he made an exception for the Princess Royal, whom he described as "Anne, Flower of Princesses".

In the autumn of 1730, a masque devised by John Rich was put on for the Princess Royal's 21st birthday in the gardens around Kew Palace when "a thousand lamps" hung from the trees.

Queen Caroline's first housekeeper at the Queen's House at Kew (pictured) was Sarah Bigge, who in 1733 married Stephen Duck, Caroline's thresher poet.

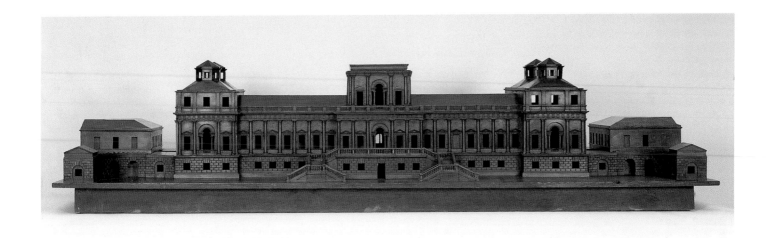

ABOVE 34. *Model of a design by William Kent for a new palace to replace Richmond Lodge. Kent designed several replacements for Richmond Lodge for George II, as did William Chambers for George III. Of all these eighteenth-century visions for a new palace, this pearwood model is the only surviving example.*

RIGHT 35. *Detail from* A New Plan of Richmond Garden *by John Rocque, 1748. Using the spoils from the building of the canal, a mound was formed at its southern end. In 1733, William Kent created a Classical temple for its summit affording views over the surrounding countryside and river, and across to Twickenham and Syon House on the opposite bank.*

36. The Family of George II *by William Hogarth, c. 1732. A unique view of the entire family of George II and Queen Caroline enjoying a panorama of Kew and the river from Kent's Tuscan temple on the mound at the southern end of the riverside terrace. Soon after this painting was finished, Kent ousted Hogarth, preventing him from undertaking further royal commissions.*

doubtful whether she or any member of her immediate family resided at the house at this time.

Queen Caroline particularly became fond of Richmond Lodge, which was settled on her at the accession, and relished the degree of privacy afforded by its small size and lack of grandeur; here she could cultivate her personal interests in the arts, literature, philosophy and theology. Moreover, the new Queen now possessed the wherewithal to translate her interest in the gardens there into action.

The grassed riverside terrace begun by the Duke of Ormonde was enhanced with a retaining wall and extended north as far as Kew. A canal was cut west of the lodge to the river terrace and the excavated earth used to create a mound on top of which a Tuscan temple was built (figs. 35, 36). The avenues were sanded or gravelled to provide walks, and Bridgeman "dared", as Horace Walpole later stated, "to introduce cultivated fields and even morsels of a forest appearance". All now served as material to enhance nature's rich landscape.

William Kent's embellishments

William Kent was commissioned to design a series of garden buildings for the new Queen. "Building a new pavilion at Richmond" is recorded in the accounts of the Office of Works as early as 1729 and it was intended to be set in the woods north of the lodge. It was furnished with a magnificent chimney piece, designed by Kent, with carving by the Italian sculptor Giovanni Battista Guelfi and engraving by Isaac Ware.

In 1730 Kent designed a more contentious garden building for Richmond. The Hermitage was a curious, rustic, Gothic structure built into a mound that sprouted a puny clump of pine trees (fig. 38). It was

38. *The Hermitage at Richmond by George III when Prince of Wales, c. 1755. This was almost certainly drawn from life; the Prince's use of a natural setting contrasts with Kent's more fanciful drawing of the same subject with mythological figures and 'Arcadia' inscribed over the doorway.*

situated in the most northerly wooded area of the estate, which Bridgeman had embellished with a diagonal Wilderness, a great oval clearing 510 feet in diameter, and an amphitheatre composed of elms on a mound just behind the new building. Alexander Pope commented, "Every man and every boy is writing verses on the royal hermitage." The *London Journal* congratulated the Queen, exclaiming that she was building "a temple in the hearts of the people of England". The *Craftsman* of 13 September 1735 provided a fuller, if perhaps biased, description:

> ... very grotesque, from being a heap of stones thrown into a very artful disorder, and curiously embellished with moss and shrubs, to represent rude Nature. The entrance of this pile is adorned with a range of iron palisades finely gilt. A person attends to open the gates to all comers. Upon entering you behold, elevated on high, a very curious Busto of the Honourable and justly celebrated Robert Boyle Esq. incompassed with Rays of Gold. On each side of him below are placed Sir Isaac Newton, Mr Locke, Dr Clarke and Mr Wollaston, author of the *Religion of Nature delineated*.

This was Caroline's own Temple of British Worthies, such as Kent was creating together with a very similar hermitage for Lord Cobham at Stowe (fig. 37). The building at Richmond held the added romance of its situation, close to the site of the fifteenth-century

39. *To swell the terrace, or to*
        sink the grot
    In all let Nature never be
        forgot.
Alexander Pope's lines on
gardening are echoed in
Merlin's Cave, built by William
Kent for Queen Caroline in
woodland to the north of
Richmond Lodge and arrived
at via a labyrinth.

40. *William Kent designed this*
small Classical building, which
stood at the end of the canal in
Richmond Gardens. It had
stucco walls and its interior was
described by a contemporary as
"furnished suitable to a royal
dairy, the utensils for the milk
being of the most beautiful
china". The building was
intended more for the delight
of the Queen than for dairy
production.

anchorite cells of the Carthusian monastery. Henry Flitcroft, the Clerk of the Works for Richmond, and Andrew Jelfe, the Works carpenter, carried out the commission. Guelfi was originally given the order to make four stone statues of Samuel Clarke, John Locke, Sir Isaac Newton and William Wollaston. By 1733 the number of busts required had risen to six with the addition of John Bacon and Robert Boyle, and Michael Rysbrack was then employed to carve them in marble. Five of these busts are now at Kensington Palace. It is probable that the bust of Bacon was never carved. Dr Clarke, who had died in 1729, was a great favourite with the Queen, and Newton a teacher to both. The inclusion of Boyle underlined the Queen's interest in natural philosophy and, set beside it, serious analytic philosophy embodied in the bust of John Locke.

The final building designed for Richmond Gardens was the most controversial. It was called Merlin's Cave or, as the *Craftsman* described it, "an old Haystack thatch'd over" (fig. 39). In 1736, Edmund Curll gave a fuller description in his *Rarities of Richmond*: "It is a thatched edifice and very gothique. The room is circular, supported by four wooden pillars, and the walls, at present bare. At each end of the room are a few books in three small niches." Its main attraction was a group of waxwork figures: Merlin, sitting at a table with his wand, books and mathematical instruments; his secretary; Elizabeth I with her nurse; Henry VII's queen, Elizabeth of York; and finally Minerva, goddess of learning and the arts (fig. 41). This "unintelligible puppet show", as Horace Walpole was to refer to it,

had its own poet-in-residence: Stephen Duck, the thresher poet, who was plucked from rural Wiltshire as an untutored early Rousseau-esque genius and offered his sycophantic verses to the Queen. In front of the entrance to Merlin's Cave, Bridgeman created an elm-covered mound and a large rectangular pond, always humorously referred to as "Duck's pond". George II most certainly did not appreciate the jest, or the cost, and berated the Queen for "such silly childish stuff". Whatever were the Queen's intentions with regard to the Hermitage and Merlin's Cave, they were probably not intended to carry an overt political message as embodied in Lord Cobham's garden buildings at Stowe, but were more patriotic, toying in a kitsch Kentian way with the prevailing arguments of the day: Classical versus Gothic; art confronting nature; Classical values and modern thinking. Perhaps the Society of Ancient Britons, founded in 1717 in Caroline's honour and periodically patronized by her, may even have provided an initial idea for the building. Certainly Caroline worked hard at establishing the Hanoverians, whose popularity was precarious, as the ruling family of Britain.

Kent also designed a fashionable dairy house to stand at the head of the canal (fig. 40), and covered seats, such as he had made for Kensington Gardens, which, according to an early guide by George Bickham, were scattered around the gardens. In another part of the gardens, possibly in the menagerie designated near the lodge on John Rocque's plan of 1748 (fig. 42), cages for tigers at a cost of £320 and

41. A section of Merlin's Cave in the royal gardens at Richmond. In addition to its waxwork figures with their obscure iconography, a select library of modern authors was installed, with volumes of Shakespeare and lines written by Stephen Duck, the thresher poet and the Queen's librarian.

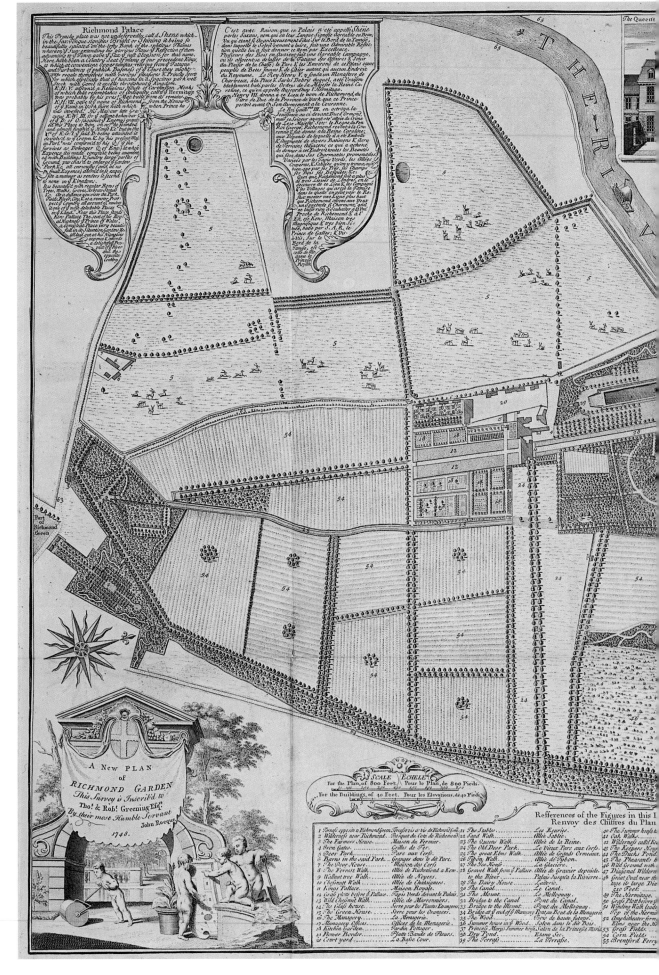

42. *John Rocque's* A New Plan of Richmond Garden, *1748. Rocque, a French cartographer, probably drew on an earlier lost map to compile this plan, which provides important information on the layout and appearance of the royal pleasure grounds. The plan was first published in 1734 and republished in 1748 and 1754, but with few amendments.*

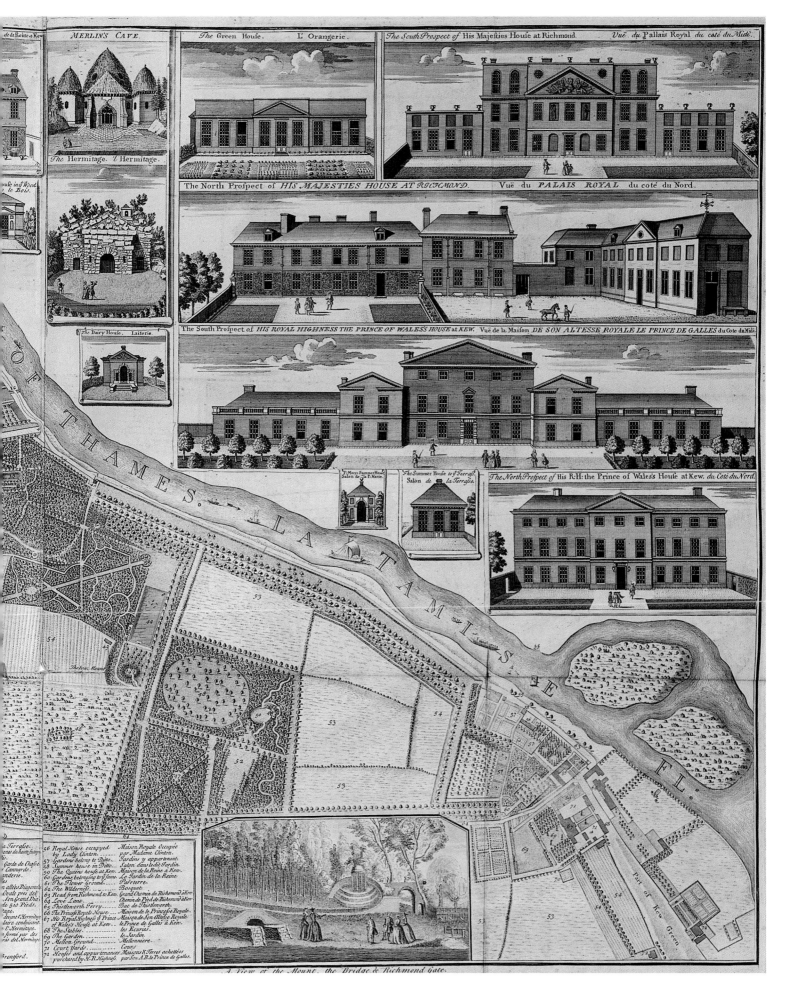

MERLIN'S CAVE.

The Green House. L'Orangerie.

The South Prospect of His Majesties House at Richmond. Vuë du Pallais Royal du coté du Midi.

The Hermitage. L'Hermitage.

The North Prospect of HIS MAJESTIES HOUSE AT RICHMOND. Vuë du PALAIS ROYAL du coté du Nord.

The Dairy House. Laiterie.

The South Prospect of HIS ROYAL HIGHNESS THE PRINCE OF WALESS HOUSE at Kew. Vuë de la Maison DE SON ALTESSE ROYALE LE PRINCE DE GALLES du Coté du Midi.

Ye Mary Summer House. Salon de la P. Marie. The Summer House to ye Terrass. Salon de la Terrasse. The North Prospect of His R:H: the Prince of Wales's House at Kew. du Coté du Nord.

THAMES. LA TAMISE FL.

56 Royal House occupyed by Lady Clinton. Maison Royale Occupée par Madame Clinton.
57 Gardens belong to Ditto. Jardins y appartenant.
58 Summer house in Ditto. Salon dans ledit Jardin.
59 The Queens house at Kew. Maison de la Reine a Kew.
60 Garden belonging to ye same. Le Jardin de la Reine
61 The Flower Ground. Parterre.
62 The Wilderness. Bosquet.
63 Road from Richmond to Kew. Grand Chemin de Richmond à Kew.
64 Love Lane. Chemin de Pied de Richmond à Kew.
65 Thistleworth Ferry. Bac de Thistleworth.
66 The Prince Royal House. Maison de le Prince le Royale.
67 His Royal Highness ye Prince of Wales's House at Kew. Maison de Son Altesse Royale le Prince de Galles à Kew.
68 The Stables. les Ecuries.
69 The Garden. le Jardin.
70 Mellow Ground. Mellonniere.
71 Court Yards. Cours.
72 Houses and appurtenances purchased by H:R:Highness. Maisons & Terres achettées par Son A.R. le Prince de Galles.

A View of the Mount, the Bridge & Richmond Gate.

39

LEFT 43. *Door-lock in the King's Breakfast Room. Seventeen of these fine brass rim-locks, which have sophisticated internal workings, survive in the palace. They are engraved with the Prince of Wales's feathers, the Garter star and the initials of Prince Frederick, suggesting that he may have lodged with the princesses during his first summer visits to Kew.*

BELOW LEFT 44. *Among several layers of wallpaper is this pretty hand-made floral sprig wallpaper (top) representing some of the oldest surviving fragments in the house. It is probably mid-eighteenth century and survives in the ante-room to the bedroom of Princess Augusta, daughter of George III, where it was pasted directly on to a plaster wall, instead of a canvas lining, as was more commonly the case.*

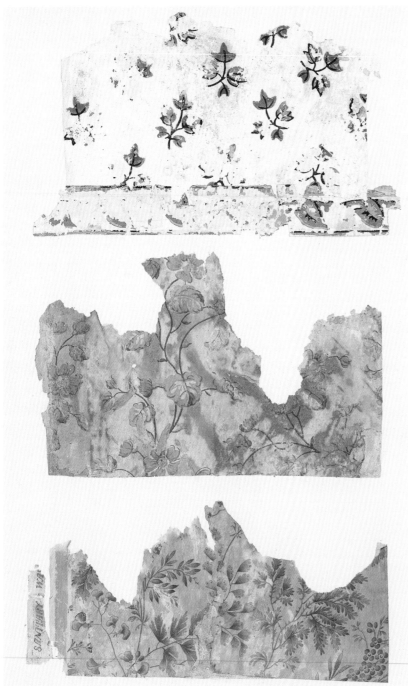

for civet cats at a more modest £20 were installed in 1727. These creatures, confined in inadequate housing, were often short-lived. They provided merely the thrill of novelty and the exotic. The 'tigers' may have been from the litter of three cubs whelped at the Tower of London menagerie in 1734.

Kew Palace reoccupied

On Lady Day 1728, Queen Caroline acquired a 99-year lease on what is now known as Kew Palace, with the intention of providing residence for her three older daughters when the court was at Richmond. The house itself affords the best evidence for the provision and modifications made for the reception of the three princesses. Remodelling seems to have been comprehensive but not indiscriminate, with some thought put into the new uses of the rooms. Work continued on a piecemeal basis into the mid-1730s. The original and by now old-fashioned windows were replaced to second-floor level with large sashes, together with modern shutters. On the ground and first floors, many of the Jacobean features were systematically stripped out and replaced; a new and elegant staircase was built, this time rising to only the second floor, lit by a lantern suspended from a gilded ceiling rose (fig. 20). On the ground floor, the spartan, functional wainscoting was replaced in the old hall, but curiously the plaster overdoor was retained, and a large stone chimney piece was added to the old panelling around the fireplace. In the common parlour (the King's Library) across the hall, the seventeenth-century panelling, overmantel and curious 'green men' were again retained and augmented with a bulky fireplace, but the windows on the west side, as elsewhere in the house, were blocked and new panelling installed (fig. 19). Most importantly, any surviving ornate and decorative painted schemes were obliterated by coats of off-whites, creams and more sober, eighteenth-century colours.

The first floor continued to form the principal living area of the house. Panelling was installed around the

45. Frederick, Prince of Wales
by Antoine Pesne, c. 1724.
This portrait was painted
at Herrenhausen, the great
Hanoverian royal palace, when
Frederick was sixteen. Lady
Mary Wortley Montagu had
visited Frederick in Hanover
and described him to Lady
Bristol as having "all the
accomplishments that it is
possible to have at his age;
with an air of sprightliness and
understanding and something
so very engaging and easy in
his behaviour that he needs
no advantage of his rank to
appear charming".

ladies attendant on the princesses, or, perhaps, as supplementary bedrooms and storage areas. One closet was divided with a curious glazed door and internal sash window, probably as a dressing room. By tradition it was a room for powdering wigs, though this has no foundation in the documentary record. The ante-room adjacent was, however, provided with floral wallpaper shortly afterwards (fig. 44).

At this time an annexe was probably added to the west, beginning an accretive process of building to house smaller kitchens, sculleries and servants' quarters. This freed up more areas of the house for residential use, and removed noxious smells and the risk of fire from the main building. Within the house, a servants' stair rose from the sculleries and the Pages' Waiting Room through the centre of the house and into the attic. On the west side of the second floor, and in the attic, many more elements of the seventeenth-century decoration were left intact, though rooms were subdivided and some early panelling, perhaps removed from the lower floor, was reset here. The attic space was enlarged by spanning across the old valleys or spaces between the original roofs, and was fitted out simply for extra capacity.

Within a few years, the house was turned from an old-fashioned Jacobean pile into a rather more elegant and severe early Georgian mansion. Internally it was ostentatious. Damask hung from the walls, rooms were provided with walnut chairs, cabinets and dressing tables, while a mahogany table was set up in the princesses' dressing and eating room on the first floor. The eldest princess had yellow curtains in her dressing room, while the bedchambers had crimson linen window curtains. Rooms were also furnished for the princesses' ladies, Lady Anne Lumley and Lady Isabella Finch, and for their pages and ordinary servants, who slept in the attics. Life at Kew Palace was seemingly agreeable, though at times provided little appeal for Princess Amelia, who commented from her apartment at Kensington Palace, "Papa and Mamma are gone again to Richmond as the custom proves to be every Wed and Sat. We stay them days comfortably at home and rest."

Prince Frederick arrives

After a perilous mid-winter journey from Hanover where, separated from his family, he had continued to live after 1714, Frederick, Prince of Wales finally set foot in England in December 1728, a few weeks before his twenty-second birthday (fig. 45). Initial impressions of public and court towards the Prince were favourable. Lady Bristol described him as "the most agreeable young man it is possible to imagine". Although George II initially considered Frederick

lower parts of the rooms, above which the walls were left plain for fabric hangings, and several fireplaces were given new and simpler veined marble surrounds. The updating of the house was not comprehensive, however. One plaster ceiling was retained, while in the Great Chamber (the Queen's Drawing Room) the impressive marble chimney piece was allowed to stay. It is possible that Richard Levett removed an ornate ceiling from this room when he installed new panelling. If similar features survived elsewhere in the house, they were removed at this time.

The second floor and attics underwent similar modification, though in simpler style, and the plainness of the wainscoting here indicates that the rooms were used for more important servants, for

46. *A group portrait of Frederick, Prince of Wales with his brother the Duke of Cumberland and five sisters by William Aikman (1682–1731). The new Prince of Wales shared many interests with Queen Caroline and the Princess Royal and, at first, positively delighted in Princess Amelia and her love of cards and gossip. He indulged his sisters, giving a ball at Kew for Amelia's and Caroline's joint birthday in 1731 and arranging after-hunt dinners.*

"not a son I need be much afraid of", the Prince's popularity soon aroused his jealousy and the characteristic Hanoverian animosity between a sovereign and his heir emerged once again. George II had himself enjoyed an allowance of £100,000 when he was Prince of Wales. Although that sum had been earmarked in the Civil List for Frederick, his father chose instead to dole out less than one quarter of that, grudgingly and in monthly instalments.

When George II made his first return to Hanover in May 1729, relations between the Prince and his family relaxed and, during the summer months of the King's absence, the Queen and her newly reassembled family were often to be found at Richmond and Kew (figs. 1, 46). Local outings and walks occupied summer days while evening entertainment invariably consisted of card parties, the players often gambling for high stakes. The Princess Royal won 500 guineas at the dice game of Hazard one evening, and in her letters to Lady Portland the lottery-ticket draw was a regular news item from Princess Amelia. But the most popular activity at Richmond was still hunting. Henrietta Howard wrote, "We hunt with great noise

and violence, and have every day a very tolerable chance to have a neck broke." Riding accidents certainly occurred even to royal princesses, although none was serious. Perhaps spurred on by the amorous Duke of Grafton, Princess Amelia became increasingly fond of hunting, on one occasion arriving at chapel in her hunting dress with a small dog tucked under each arm.

The Princess Royal was an accomplished musician, and was a pupil of Handel. This was reflected in the palace, where the first-floor drawing room was designated the princesses' music room and lavishly decorated and furnished with green silk taffeta window curtains, expensive armchairs covered in green damask, and six square stools, all trimmed with gilt nails. Between the windows were elegant pier tables with marble tops and above them large mirrors in carved and gilded frames, made by Benjamin Goodison. In the autumn of 1733, a great flurry of activity took place within the princesses' house at Kew. The Princess Royal had received an offer of marriage from the Prince of Orange – a choice that John, Lord Hervey (fig. 57) pointed out was one between Holland or the hell of the "St James's convent [St James's

47. *Frontispiece of* Two
Historical Accounts ... of New
Forest and Richmond New
Park *depicting a bound-beating
party of Richmond Parish,
16 May 1751. Princess Amelia
tried to exclude public access
to Richmond Park when she
became ranger there in spring
1751. She declared, "The world
must be coming to an end when
the vulgar dared thus to keep
standing on their rights in
defiance of a Princess." Horace
Walpole commented that it
brought to mind the occasion
when her mother asked his
father how much it would
cost to shut the public out of
St James's Park; his reply:
"Only a crown, Ma'am."*

Palace]". Anne chose Holland. The marriage was to have been in November but the Prince of Orange caught a chill and was forced to convalesce in Bath, so the wedding did not take place until March 1734.

The Prince of Orange may have briefly savoured the elegant interiors of Kew Palace, for it was possibly to the palace that the young couple repaired for a short honeymoon before they set sail for Holland. The Prince of Wales, who had just taken a lease on the house across the road, took a hand in the celebrations, plaiting the horses' manes with orange ribbons and organizing beer, bonfires and fireworks for the occasion.

After the departure of the Oranges to Holland, it is doubtful whether Princess Caroline spent much time at Kew Palace. A retiring character with uncertain health, she kept close to her mother and retired to St James's Palace altogether after the Queen's death in 1737. Princess Amelia, however, was of a very different temperament. She was independent and often outspoken. Early negotiations for a union with Prince Frederick of Prussia did not materialize and she never married, although there was much gossip about her liaison with the Duke of Grafton. George II granted her the rangership of Richmond Park, which she took up at the death of Lord Orford in 1751 (fig. 47). The position also gave her the use of the new lodge, known as White Lodge, where she made alterations, notably the addition of two wings. Kew Palace, which she abandoned at this time, must have begun to look rather old-fashioned compared to the elegance of this delightful retreat.

FREDERICK *and Augusta* 1730–51

Frederick, Prince of Wales moves to Kew. His far-reaching ideas for his family and the estate are strongly to influence the gardens at Kew and the ideas of the succeeding reign.

48. Frederick, Prince of Wales, with the Knights of the Round Table (detail) by Charles Philips (1708–47). This may be the only view of the interior of the White House. Over the fireplace can be seen Wootton's portrait of the Princess Royal in hunting dress, which is recorded at the White House in the Blue Room. However, this particular room cannot be positively identified.

49. Designed in 1732 by William Kent for Frederick, Prince of Wales the royal barge sported a gilded dolphin as a figurehead while further dolphins and mermaids with the royal crest and acanthus leaves decorated the stern. The cabin with its heraldic painted ceiling was upholstered in green velvet. The crew wore specially designed livery with large silver badges. The barge was often accompanied by a musical escort. It can now be seen at the National Maritime Museum in London.

Prince Frederick's quest for a country home

In the honeymoon period following his arrival in England, Frederick, for a time, delighted in the company of his newly discovered family. It does not, therefore, appear surprising that he wished to have a house in close proximity both to his sisters and to his parents' house in the adjoining estate at Richmond. He had already purchased Carlton House as his London home and had a very beautiful and extravagant royal barge, designed by William Kent, to ferry him to Kew (fig. 49).

The largest house at Kew, which stood opposite Kew Palace, was at this time unoccupied (fig. 50). Kew House, as it was known, had passed from Henry Capel's widow, Dorothy, at her death in 1721 to their great-niece, Lady Elizabeth Capel. Elizabeth had married Samuel Molyneux, secretary to George II, then Prince of Wales, and an enthusiastic astronomer. It was in an observatory perched on top of this house in 1727 that Molyneux and James Bradley, the Astronomer Royal, had made important observations on the aberration of light with their Newtonian telescope. Molyneux died suddenly at the age of thirty-eight and Lady Elizabeth caused a scandal by immediately eloping with her husband's doctor, Nathaniel St André, whom she married in 1730. It would be surprising if Frederick had not cast a wistful glance at this desirable house with its mature gardens and observatory in the attic.

Negotiations with the St Andrés for possession of the house may well have been initiated during

Frederick enjoyed family birthday entertainments. In 1740, his eldest daughter's third birthday was celebrated, with a masque, featuring 'Rule Britannia' specially composed by Thomas Arne (pictured).

Prince Frederick was enchanted with his new wife and addressed a poem to her that ended with the lines: "That grace with which you look and speak and move; That thus has set my soul on fire."

The thirteen marble statues by Francavilla ordered for Frederick's gardens at Kew arrived after his death and remained crated up in their packing cases for sixty years. Four were later installed at Hampton Court Palace.

50. This reconstruction, based on archaeological and documentary evidence, shows the area around Kew Palace in 1785. The present palace is dwarfed by the larger and grander White House, flanked to the left by its kitchen and laundry and to the right by the stables, which had been extended in the 1770s. The building to the far left is the Queen's House, in all likelihood a late seventeenth-century structure, which was demolished around 1802 to make way for George III's Castellated Palace. Of this group, only the main block of Kew Palace, the kitchens and the small housekeeper's residence adjoining survive today. Illustration: Jonathan Foyle.

Frederick's first visits to Kew. Soon he was paying rent on the house, now designated "His Royal Highness's House at Kew". Preparatory building work began in the summer of 1730 and the Prince even ordered a billiard table in February of that year. In March 1731 he purchased the contents of the house from Nathaniel St André for £720. 8s. 6d. At the same time he also purchased, for an additional £236. 19s., furniture from a coach house on Kew Green that had belonged to Henry, Earl of Thomond. Known as the Little House, this dwelling may also have been used by the Prince himself. The lease for the estate, which included both houses, was officially granted to James Pelham for Frederick, Prince of Wales on 11 September 1731.

Frederick at the White House

In the first year, Kew House was remodelled considerably and initial bills from various workmen survive totalling almost £1200, though with further fitting out and finishing the cost rose to over £8000 by 1735 – far short of the expense estimated for a wholly new mansion. The architect was William Kent, assisted by his comptroller Thomas Ripley. As a painter by training and inclination, but a far better architect in terms of skill, Kent had transformed Kensington Palace for George II. He was also a talented garden designer with links to Lord Burlington, the advocate and patron of the Palladian style in England.

As his first major architectural commission, Kew House was a highly important and transitional building for Kent. Externally the result was frigidly Palladian, with the most spartan articulation, but on to the old house he attached an impressive south elevation. The whole structure was rendered and whitewashed and was subsequently known as the White House (fig. 51). Internally, Kent's creativity and imagination were given free rein and here he created rooms of dazzling extravagance, which were held to be comparable to the grandest houses of the day. However, evidence for this sumptuous interior is meagre (fig. 48). William Chambers later provided a description of the building and the renewal of the lease in 1759 also gives clues, but the picture remains frustratingly confusing.

The centre of the house may have been contrived

from an earlier courtyard. It rose to two storeys with seven-foot high panelling, lit by upper windows, and was called a great hall. To the south a passage cut right through the house, crossing the stair vestibule, which itself was panelled and possibly had a decorated ceiling. To the west lay some of the Prince's more sumptuous state rooms. An antechamber, drawing room and cabinet led to a gallery. The cabinet, we are told, was furnished with panels of 'Japan' (imitation lacquerwork), probably reflecting the extraordinary sum of £139 paid to Mr Riorto in 1731 "for japanning the closet". An ornate ceiling and chimney piece in this room were also by Kent. The principal room was the gallery, which seems to have been painted blue on the walls and panelling – a most ostentatious and expensive colour for the time – complete with gilded decorations and a star and garter on the ceiling. Landscape paintings by John Ellis and six portraits by William Hogarth, commissioned at fifteen guineas apiece, hung on the walls. For this room Michael Rysbrack provided busts and tables of marble. The effect was rich and inspiration

may have been drawn from Lord Burlington's Blue Velvet Room at Chiswick House, completed with Kent's collaboration only a few years before (fig. 53).

In the eastern part of the house the more important servants, such as the bedchamber women, had a drawing room, hung with paintings and embellished by another Kent ceiling. On the upper floor, a second gallery had been decorated with grotesque work by Kent and a drawing room likewise, described as being "in party colours and gold", with a central tablet picturing the mythological story of Leda and the Swan. Paintings by Veronese, Albano and Claude Lorraine hung on its green silk walls. Frederick's own private quarters were equally sumptuous, with yet more ceilings above panelling and a dressing room fitted up like a *Schatzkammer*, or cabinet of curiosities, with japanned cabinets, Meissen porcelain and objects of ivory and amber. Minor embellishments, such as cornices, were carved by Isaac Mansfield and probably gilded by John Jones, who also gilded the doorcases. A single door from one of these rooms survives, now reused in the Great Kitchen. It has rich

BELOW 51. *Elevations of the north and south fronts of the White House by William Chambers, 1763. These drawings pay homage to William Kent's transformation of an earlier building on the site. On both sides, the building was proportioned according to strict Palladian principles, with minimal embellishment.*

BOTTOM 52. *The layout of the White House, after William Chambers, 1763. An older house to the north (bottom, right of centre) was retained as a lodge, while flanking it a new mews was built. To the west (right) lie the kitchens within a separate courtyard, which also contained a still-room, brew-house and laundry.*

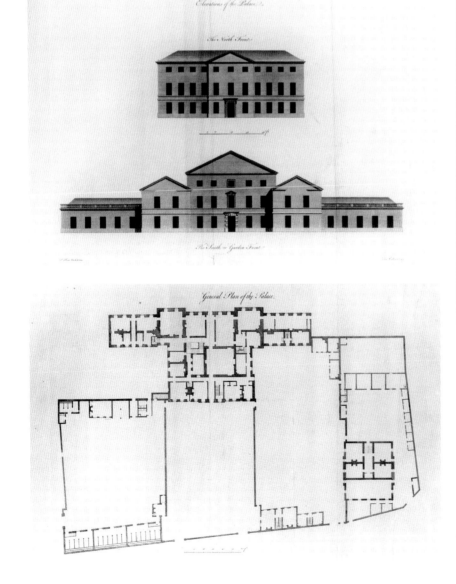

53. *The Blue Velvet Room at Chiswick House, where William Kent introduced a blue and gold scheme in the same way as he did at the White House just a few years later. Chiswick, built in 1729 by Lord Burlington, drew on designs by Palladio and Scamozzi. Kent assisted in the design of the interiors and the gardens.*

embellishments, with egg-and-dart and bead-and-reel mouldings, contrasting with the elegant simplicity of Kew Palace.

All this splendour has disappeared but, remarkably, Frederick's Great Kitchen survives much as it did when first constructed. It is characterized externally by the symmetrical and Classical proportions that would have been demanded at the time, preserving great subtlety in the articulation of its brick – showing the more expensive bond and better quality on the public side; yet it was provided with a layout and attention to detail that show an interest in the rational and logical interpretation of design (fig. 54).

Family life at Kew

In 1736, Frederick married Augusta of Saxe-Gotha. The prospect of the new bride gave added impetus to completing the furnishing of the White House. Frederick had purchased the furniture and furnish-ings of the Molyneux house, but still changed and added considerably. The large central hall now contained two great carved marble vases and on the walls hung portraits of kings and statesmen, including those of William III and Mary II. To the west, in the state apartments, the drawing room was hung with tapestries and royal portraits. The second floor accommodated servants and the observatory, while the equerries occupied the wings.

The household expanded apace, and there was an extra push to complete and fit out the kitchens, with the usual extravagance. Enormous amounts of equipment were provided, from copper chocolate-pots and sugar hatchets to coffee-mills, a vast array of pans, skillets and cauldrons, spice boxes, mincing knives and even lark spits. The first list of salaries to survive shows that there were twenty-eight servants employed in the kitchens alone, from the Master Cook, Joseph Harper Reynolds, paid the princely

Holbein sketches in a bureau at Kensington Palace and hung them at Richmond Lodge. She peopled Richmond Park "with shepherds and shepherdesses" for a *fête champêtre*, while Frederick appeared for a masquerade dressed "after a drawing of Kent's in green waistcoat, leopard skin and quivers, with caps and feathers upon the head like a Harry the 8th by Holbein".

Yet despite the convergence in the interests and activities of Queen and Prince at Richmond and Kew, their personal relationship was becoming soured. This state of affairs resulted from the suspicions entertained towards the Prince by the King, whom the Queen unfailingly obeyed, and from the venomous animosity felt towards the Prince by Lord Hervey, with whom the Queen constantly chatted (fig. 57).

By 1737, Frederick had still not been granted his full allowance and was now greatly in debt. He had further angered the King by fraternizing with the Opposition. The Prince and Lord Hervey, who had been close friends, had had a great falling out in 1732, ostensibly occasioned by their tangled relationships with Anne Vane, one of the Queen's maids of honour. From this point, Hervey gradually turned into the Prince's most implacable enemy and became instrumental in fostering the coldness that subsequently developed between the Prince and his parents.

In the summer of 1737, Princess Augusta was expecting their first child, which George II insisted be

salary of £100 a year, to the poor turn-broaches, who spent their time turning spits of meat and roasting themselves equally by the great range, which still survives.

Relations between the Queen and Prince Frederick

The early 1730s were a time of great activity in the Richmond and Kew estates, with Kent and Rysbrack amongst others working concurrently in both. There is no evidence to suggest any formulated collaboration between the Queen and Frederick, yet some seeds of influence, or cross-pollination, must surely have blown across Love Lane, the public road that divided Richmond Gardens from Kew Gardens. As Caroline was setting out a menagerie for deer and wild beasts at Richmond, the Prince was acquiring antelopes and other exotic animals, including a quagga, at Kew (fig. 56). Queen Caroline discovered a cache of

RIGHT 56. *Prince Frederick's quagga. The quagga was a sub-species of the plains zebra, which was striped only on its forequarters. It was once abundant in southern Africa but was hunted to extinction. The last living example died in 1883. This specimen was brought from the Cape of Good Hope and lived for a while at Kew. The drawing was made from its skin.*

born in the palace in which he was residing. On the evening of 31 July, when Augusta went into premature labour, this happened to be Hampton Court. However, she was rushed away by Frederick to St James's Palace, where she almost instantly gave birth to a daughter, Augusta. For this disobedience, on 11 September George II banished his son from his palaces with almost the same restrictions as had been imposed by his father upon him as Prince of Wales in 1717, except that the new baby remained with her parents.

On 12 September, Frederick took his wife and baby to Kew. From here the new mother penned submissive letters of justification for Frederick's behaviour to George II, which served only to increase his fury against his son. Hervey's reports of the Queen "wishing a hundred times a day that the Prince might drop down dead of an apoplexy, cursing the hour of his birth and the Princess Caroline declaring she grudged him every hour he continued to breathe, and reproaching Lord Hervey with his weakness for ever having loved him" reveal the extent of Hervey's venom. What the Queen's deepest feelings were cannot be known but the breach between mother and son remained unhealed. Queen Caroline died in November 1737 without again seeing her eldest son or meeting Frederick's second child, her grandson, who was born the following year and who would become George III.

Frederick as the country gentleman

Rarely setting foot in any of the royal palaces, Frederick now lived his life rather as a noble country gentleman. Augusta's Lady of the Bedchamber, Lady Ann Irwin, related:

> I passed a fortnight at Kew very agreeably; the Prince lives there quite in private, without form; passes his time wholly with his family, whom he treats in so obliging a manner and with such an easy familiarity as makes the attendance very agreeable ... We are admitted to share all their diversions, viz. music, play, walking, and whatever amusements can be thought of in the country in a large family of men and women.

Frederick created a world full of entertainment, learning and fun for his children, which would deeply influence them, especially his eldest son, George. Dr John Theophilus Desaguliers, Frederick's chaplain and a natural philosopher, moved into the White House. In the attic observatory with a planetarium at one end and space for mechanical and mathematical instruments at the other, he gave daily lectures to the household on astronomy and experimental philosophy, at the same time forming an occasional masonic lodge there.

The children took part in plays, in which visitors

ABOVE 57. *John, Lord Hervey, Queen Caroline's Vice-Chamberlain, took outrageous liberties with the Queen that she would not have tolerated from any other quarter. His diary of court life, written in the third person, reports intimate conversations that can rarely be corroborated. Princess Amelia loathed him but her sister Caroline was infatuated with him. Alexander Pope referred to him as a "bug with gilded wings".*

58. *A Man doing the Splits by George Dance, c. 1760–90. High spirits and boisterous fun were essential components of Frederick's entertainments for himself and his family.*

59. Frederick, Prince of Wales, out stag-hunting *by John Wootton and William Hogarth, c. 1745. Frederick acquired an additional house, Park Place at Henley, expressly for hunting. While at Kew, he hunted in Richmond Park.*

60. Cricket in the Artillery Ground *by Francis Hayman, 1743. Frederick both played and enjoyed watching cricket and taught it to his children. He may well have captained a Surrey team on Kew Green, where cricket matches are still played today. An earlier injury from a cricket ball to his chest was reported to have hastened his death after he caught pneumonia in March 1751.*

weavers at Spitalfields. Birthdays were always celebrated with plays, concerts, conjurors, bonfires and fireworks. For Prince George's eleventh birthday, the Prince offered a silver cup for the winning oarsman in a race on the river. Frederick and Augusta attended in the Kentian barge while George was given a Venetian gondola, complete "with watermen dressed in Chinese habits". Frederick wrote stories, plays and poetry and patronized the local poets including James Thomson, author of the highly successful *Seasons*.

Lord Bute and the gardens at Kew

In 1747, Frederick met John Crichton Stuart, 3rd Earl of Bute (1713–1792) at the races in Egham and soon discovered their shared enthusiasms for architecture, books, paintings, music and above all botany. Bute became a Gentleman of the Bedchamber and indispensable to the household (fig. 61). With Bute's assistance, Frederick began collecting and cultivating plants, many of them exotics, and with renewed enthusiasm planning new landscapes at Kew. It was "a compleat place, very beautiful in the situation, gardens and all laid out at His Highness's expence", recorded Rocque on his 1748 plan of the estate (fig. 42). Certainly there are records of orders placed for flowering plants, including geraniums, wallflowers, marigolds, roses and jasmine, and bulbs, such as crocus, narcissus, snowdrops and ranunculus, by the thousand. Additionally, trees were planted which included English elms, yews, pines, laurels and hornbeams and ornamental trees such as birch, cherry, laburnum and myrtle. A kitchen garden and melon ground appear close to the White House on Rocque's plan.

Frederick visited Alexander Pope across the river, supplying urns for his garden and assimilating his painterly notions of gardening. Then there were the influences of Lord Burlington's estate at Chiswick and, especially, Lord Cobham's gardens at Stowe. Frederick had kept on the estate gardener, John Dillman, who lived on Kew Green. However, no plan of Frederick's intentions for the landscaping of the gardens survives. There is no evidence to suggest that Kent had a direct hand in the landscape design but his influence is discernible. Kent had first introduced *chinoiserie* inside the White House. Joseph Goupy, Frederick's 'cabinet-painter', now designed a Chinese summerhouse, the House of Confucius, for the gardens and a Chinese arch was also erected (fig. 63). George Vertue, the engraver and antiquary, whom Frederick asked to supply drawings for busts, provides some information on the landscape planning. He wrote that the Prince was to create a mound, a new Parnassus to be adorned with busts of ancient and modern philosophers; it was to be his Temple of Worthies at Kew. The excavated

61. John Stuart, 3rd Earl of Bute *by Sir Joshua Reynolds, 1773. Frederick had described Bute as "a fine showy man who would make an excellent ambassador in a court where there was no business", but both Frederick and his family had a high regard for this serious, pompous but loyal Scot.*

were often coerced into participating. More boisterous games were ninepins, rounders, billiards and cricket, of which Frederick was especially fond (fig. 60). The children had their own pets, and parrots in cages in the bedchambers. Alexander Pope brought the Prince a puppy from his own bitch Bounce with a collar inscribed:

I am His Highness's dog at Kew:
Pray tell me sir,
whose dog are you?

There were outings to see gypsies on several occasions, to fairs, to visit manufactories and the silk

62. Hartwell House, the Bowling Green and Octagon Pond from the North *by Balthasar Nebot, c. 1738. Other people's gardens were always a fascination for a prince constructing his own. Stowe, Chiswick, Claremont and Gubbins (Hertfordshire) were among those Frederick visited. Sir Roy Strong has suggested that the Knight of the Garter in this painting may well be Frederick on a visit to Sir Thomas Lee at Hartwell in 1737. An equestrian statue of the Prince by Henry Cheere still stands outside the house, now a hotel, in Aylesbury, Buckinghamshire.*

area would form a lake. George Bubb Dodington, erstwhile counsellor to the Prince, grumbled that in February 1750 all men, women and children were hard at work in the new walk at Kew and that there was only a cold dinner (fig. 64). When Vertue visited Kew in October later that year, he found the Prince "directing the plantation of trees and exoticks with workmen". He walked with him for two or three hours, "seeing his plantations, told his contrivances, designs of his improvements in the gardens, water works, canal", and Vertue commented on the great number of people working in the gardens and saw the new Chinese summerhouse. Goupy made a drawing of a Grecian building to be placed upon the mound. Work did not begin on the busts for the Temple of Worthies, but there was already sculpture in the gardens. Eight stone terms had been ordered in 1735, some from Rysbrack, some for the gardens

of Carlton House. Marble statues were put on plinths both in the gardens and in the courtyard in front of the White House. In 1751 an order was placed via Horace Mann in Florence for thirteen marble statues by Francavilla from the Villa Bracci.

Frederick never saw these statues arrive at Kew, nor did he see the realization of his own Temple of Worthies, for in March 1751, after spending a day working in the gardens at Kew, he caught pneumonia and died. In 1749 he had written a letter to be given to his eldest son, George, after his death. In it he implored George to pay back his father's debts and never to live above his income. For all his faults, Frederick had an amiable quality that was attractive. Mrs Clayton, later Lady Sundon, wrote of him: "he had that accessibility of manner which gives such an unspeakable charm to royalty".

64. George Bubb
Dodington *(1691–1762)*
by George Townshend,
4th Viscount and 1st Marquess
Townshend, 1751–58. Dodington
spoke of himself as "in power a
servant, out of power a friend".
Fickle holder of political office
and a sometime favourite with
Frederick, Prince of Wales he
visited Carlton House, Cliveden
and Kew. His diary records
taking part in theatrical
performances there and outings
with the royal family. On more
than one occasion he was the
butt of the Prince's practical
jokes, to which he submitted
with good humour.

65. *Engraving by*
William Woollett showing
brushing and scything at
Carlton House gardens, 1760.
It is unclear whether William
Kent had a direct hand in
Frederick's gardens at Kew
but he certainly designed the
gardens for him at Carlton
House, one of the Prince's
London homes. The terms in the
background can now be seen in
the garden behind Kew Palace.

The Making *of* KEW *Gardens* 1751–63

While raising the heir to the throne, Princess Augusta, with William Chambers and the Earl of Bute, creates gardens of international repute at Kew. "What was once a desart is now an Eden."

66. The Temple of Victory, *after George Ernest Papendiek, published 1820. This was reputedly built in one night to celebrate the Prussian and Hanoverian victory over the French at the Battle of Minden in August 1759, during the Seven Years' War.*

67. George, Prince of Wales *by Jean-Etienne Liotard (1702–1789). The young Prince of Wales was encouraged in the study of architecture, first by Bute, then with formal lessons in architectural drawing from Chambers. He must have followed with interest Chambers's early garden buildings as they were erected at Kew. Among the Prince's architectural drawings is a design for a small Classical temple.*

Princess Augusta alone

At Frederick's sudden death, Princess Augusta was pregnant with their last daughter, Caroline Matilda. The Prince had encouraged Augusta to share his interest in botany and with the help of Lord Bute she was to bring this passion to bloom at Kew. She lived up to her nickname of Princess Prudence by immediately burning her husband's papers and by calling on the King for his "paternal love and royal protection". She did this so winningly that George II volunteered to propose her as regent during the minority of her eldest son, the new Prince of Wales and future George III. Prince George (fig. 67) was almost thirteen when his father died. "I feel it here", he said, pointing to his heart, "as I did when the workmen fell from the scaffold at Kew". He was immature for his age and when the King proposed giving him a separate establishment at Kensington at the age of sixteen he was horrified. Augusta, in submissive letters, managed to keep George with her for a considerable part of the year, completely isolated from the metropolis at the family home in Kew.

The household was not without its domestic and intellectual interests. The Earl of Bute now became to a large extent instrumental in developing the tastes of the family, particularly those of Prince George, who formed an emotional and needy relationship with Bute, what might be described as a 'crush'. On reaching his eighteenth year, George implored the King to make Bute his Groom of the Stool, a request authorized with great reluctance. Bute was pompous

and lacked Frederick's sociability and common touch, yet his interests in botany, architecture, science and astronomy were serious.

Many customs introduced by Frederick were retained. Birthdays were still celebrated in the grand style (fig. 70) and after Frederick's death Augusta continued to visit Stephen Hales in nearby Teddington,

Frederick built a witch house at Kew. The little we know of it suggests it was a rustic farmhouse with a locked barn but how it was used remains a mystery.

William Chambers was knighted in 1771 by the King of Sweden for a series of drawings of Kew Gardens. George III allowed him to use the title in England.

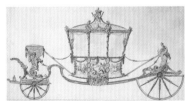

George III began his reign by commissioning William Chambers and Joseph Wilton to create a lavishly carved and gilded state coach for his coronation, a function it performs to the present day.

I AUGUSTA, B.1737 (afterwards Duchess of Brunswick), D.1813.   IV CAROLINE, B.1741   D.1759.   AUGUSTA OF SAXE-GOTHA, PRINCESS OF WALES B.1719. D.1772.   VII LOUISA, B.1749.   D.1768.
II GEORGE, B.1738 (afterwards George III)   V WILLIAM HENRY, B.1743 (afterwards Duke of Gloucester) D.1805.   VIII FREDERICK WILLIAM, B.175

68. The Family of Frederick, Prince of Wales *by George Knapton, 1751. Augusta holds her daughter Caroline Matilda, born two months after Frederick's death. George, now Prince of Wales, sits on the left and shows a plan of fortifications to his brother Edward, Duke of York. From his portrait, Frederick posthumously points down to his family. The White House at Kew can be seen in the background.*

69. Augusta, Princess of Wales *by Allan Ramsay, c. 1760. As she grew older, the Dowager Princess Augusta spent less time at Kew, visiting only to breakfast twice a week with her son George III and his family. For the rest of the time she kept to her London residence, Carlton House, where she died in February 1772.*

ABOVE 70. *For the Prince of Wales's seventeenth birthday in 1755, a pleasure barge shaped like a great swan was built by John Rich and launched on the lake at Kew, its "feet so artfully contrived as to supply the place of oars".*

71. *A silhouette portrait of Stephen Charles Triboudet Demainbray (1710–1782). Demainbray gave public lectures on natural philosophy and became tutor to the Prince of Wales (later George III). He was also appointed King's Astronomer to George III at his observatory at Kew.*

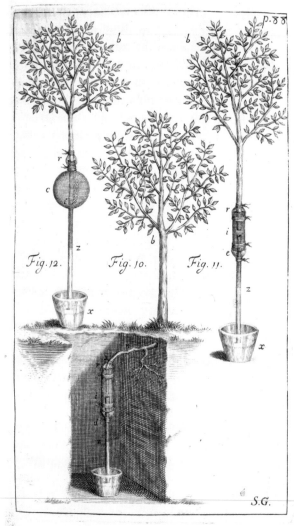

RIGHT 72. *"Up the Trunks of Trees: Investigation of the way Sap is Drawn" by Stephen Hales, 1727. Curate of Teddington, chaplain to Princess Augusta and author of* Vegetable Staticks, *Hales was a botanist and inventor and advised on the heating of Chambers's Great Stove at Kew. He conducted experiments at the Princess's house, installing a fire grate "with its lower part a foot above the mantle-piece" to measure the effect on the draught and ventilation of the room. From this beginning, Hales went on to introduce ventilation to ships of the royal navy and to the nation's hospitals and prisons.*

as she had done with her husband. Hales, a physiologist and clergyman, was appointed her Clerk of the Closet and advised her on plants (fig. 72). He was also a scientist and inventor, keen to improve the functioning of the ice house at Kew and introduce new recipes for making ices. On one occasion, he inspected and dissected a turtle on the White House kitchen table prior to its ultimate destination – the soup tureen. Stephen Demainbray replaced Desaguliers as lecturer to the royal household on natural and experimental philosophy (fig. 71). In a letter to Bute, Prince George added the postscript, "My mother has desired me to acquaint you that she is busy reading the doctrine of shocking electricity."

The education of the princes

These episodes must have enlivened a stimulating backdrop for the more formal education of the Prince of Wales and his brother Prince Edward, which took place at Kew Palace. Frederick had appointed Lord North as governor to supervise the education of his two eldest sons, with Dr Ayscough (fig. 73) as their tutor and religious instructor, George Lewis Scott, a man of high academic ability, to teach mathematics, Monsieur Dunoyer for dancing and Signor Angelo to teach them fencing. Their father had taken a lively interest in their education, exhorting them to write to him every week and tell him what they were reading. After his death it appeared

that George, although competent in composing Latin verse, was not a fluent reader. Lord Harcourt was then brought in as governor, with Thomas Hayter and Andrew Stone, formerly an able government secretary; only Scott was retained from the previous régime. The new appointments were short-lived. Harcourt complained to the King that Stone and Scott were Jacobites and threatened to resign unless they were dismissed. Harcourt and Hayter resigned, and Lord Waldegrave was brought in as the new governor.

By 1754, Kew Palace was designated on Rocque's plan of the estate as the "House of the Prince of Wales". The principal rooms were sumptuously refurbished for the use of the young boys. There were green silk window curtains throughout, gilt tables and mahogany furniture covered with green silk damask and finished with rows of double gilt nails. There was little space for servants' accommodation, but there was a pages' waiting room and a room for Mrs Tunstall, the housekeeper. At the same time the younger princes, William and Henry, had similar provision at a house on Kew Green, which was decorated with new wallpapers with fashionable patterns such as 'Gothic Temple', 'Carnation Twirle', 'Bertie Sprig' and 'Fitz Roy', ordered from the firm of Crompton and Spinnage. Their house also sported a billiard room and a newly constructed colonnade for their fencing lessons.

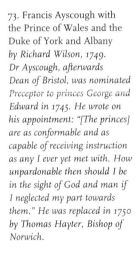

73. Francis Ayscough with the Prince of Wales and the Duke of York and Albany *by Richard Wilson, 1749. Dr Ayscough, afterwards Dean of Bristol, was nominated Preceptor to princes George and Edward in 1745. He wrote on his appointment: "[The princes] are as conformable and as capable of receiving instruction as any I ever yet met with. How unpardonable then should I be in the sight of God and man if I neglected my part towards them." He was replaced in 1750 by Thomas Hayter, Bishop of Norwich.*

The Mandarin of the Nine Whiskers – William Chambers at Kew

In 1757, Lord Bute introduced Princess Augusta to the person who would begin the ambitious architectural 'embellishments' of her garden – Sir William Chambers (1726–1796). The meteoric rise of Chambers was in no small part because of the royal favour shown him as a court architect, bestowed on him through a combination of luck and shrewd self-promotion, but ultimately for his genuine talent. Lord Bute recognized his unmistakable gifts as an architect and designer. A remarkable series of drawings survives for a grandiose mausoleum to Prince Frederick at Kew, which, though never adopted, endeared him to the widowed Augusta, who called on him to modify and add to the splendour of the royal pleasure grounds in an almost constant round of alterations and embellishment that took place from 1758 to 1763. From here he launched a lucrative commercial practice and secured lasting influence as tutor to the young George, Prince of Wales, which was to blossom fully once his pupil had become king. Chambers was well travelled and was clearly a rising star in the architectural profession.

As a young and impressionable man learning the trade, Chambers embarked on a series of voyages to China, beginning with one in 1742 by way of the Cape of Good Hope and Bengal, and as a result he became an authority on the subject of all things Chinese. After returning from his last voyage in 1748 he may have made his first royal connections by being called to Kew to advise on Joseph Goupy's designs for the House of Confucius. He did not stay long, however, and soon departed to hone his skills at the Ecole des Arts in Paris, before spending five formative years in Rome. By 1755, Robert Adam considered that "though his taste is more architectonic than Picturesque ... he both knows well and draws exquisitely". This was combined with growing confidence, as a number of lavishly illustrated architectural treatises were produced at the expense of his patrons. In 1756 he published *Designs for Chinese Buildings*, an authoritative account that was based on the shakiest of foundations, considering that Chambers was not allowed to venture further than the European trading concessions of Canton, but the book was nonetheless influential and gained wide currency in both England and France. The following year he presented a *Treatise on Civil Architecture* and was elected to the Royal Society of Arts. His transition to royal patronage as the architect to Princess Augusta and tutor to the young Prince thus seemed a natural step.

Once Chambers had been employed, Augusta's demands were relentless. The architect complained that "the prince employs me three mornings a week to teach him architecture; the building and other decorations at Kew fill up the remaining time. The princess has the rest of the week, which is scarcely sufficient as she is forever adding new embellishments at Kew, all of which I direct the execution, measure the work." Between them, in the space of just a few years, Kew was transformed and Augusta's budding 'Elysium' enhanced to new and yet more romantic heights.

Observations of the gardens
During those years, new routes and gardens were developed and peppered with an assortment of follies, building on Augusta's earlier and more modest efforts. Count Kielmansegge, the German diplomat, recorded in his diary in 1761–66:

> There is much to see in it in the way of summer houses, some of which are being built. There are close upon twenty such little buildings. In the gardens are also fine hothouses and oranges, an enclosure of wooden lattice-work for pheasants and other rare birds, a large aviary, a temple dedicated to the Sun ... a touriquet or house which turns around and round on a pivot.

Kielmansegge, like many others, was charmed by this novel treatment of a garden. On a gentle stroll, the visitor could encounter thought-provoking temples, monuments and other follies: structures that were picturesque as well as secluded, delighting the eye when happened upon through carefully contrived vistas, plantings and serpentine paths, evoking the type of English garden about which Empress Catherine the Great of Russia waxed so effusive in her correspondence with the philosopher Voltaire. Little galleries for the display of the arts or the illumination of antiquities appealed to the intellect, while some were merely disguises for garden seats or shelters from the rain. At the southern, more remote extremity of the estate, all corners of the world were encapsulated in one broad sweep, in an almost sublime trinity of mosque, pagoda and Alhambra. An eighteenth-century earthly and heavenly paradise was concocted within this confined space and Chambers was responsible, either directly or by adapting the designs of others, for this whole, extravagant stage-set.

Little of Chambers's creation has survived. The historic accounts are slender but, ultimately, many of these buildings were not physically robust. Kielmansegge marvelled that "all of these buildings consist of wood only, but are so cleverly covered with

ABOVE 76. *Smeaton's Water Engine, after George Ernest Papendiek, published 1820. John Smeaton (1724–1792) is regarded as the founder of the profession of civil engineering in Britain. In 1759 he won the Royal Society's Copley Medal for research into the mechanics of water-wheels and windmills. Kew needed an adequate water supply, so in 1763 Smeaton designed a steam engine to turn a twenty-four-foot Archimedes screw to lift water from a well. The future American presidents John Adams and Thomas Jefferson made trips to Kew to visit this modern marvel.*

RIGHT 77. *A Victorian view of the Temple of the Sun. Constructed in 1761, this was raised on a plinth with fluted columns and Corinthian capitals. The interior, protected by conventional sash windows, had its dome emblazoned with a sun in splendour, its rays reaching a frieze enriched with swags, festoons of fruit and flowers, and symbols of the zodiac.*

plaster and painted in oil colours that you could swear they were solid buildings of quarry stone, unless by knocking them you discovered the truth". He added, "I can well believe that these wooden structures will not last long, but this was not the Prince's object." Of the whole collection, fewer than half a dozen survive today.

From Ancient Greece to the Orient

In the years following the succession of George III in 1760, the gardens reached a harmonious culmina-tion with buildings and planting. Close to Kew Palace lies one of the few survivors, the Orangery, an elegant rendered building sporting gigantic windows, which was ultimately to prove a failure as an environment in which citrus fruits could thrive. From here, the eighteenth-century visitor would turn eastwards towards the little Classical Temple of the Sun (fig. 77), enclosed within its own grove, adjoining the Great Stove, which heated the greenhouse. The sur-rounding area was busy and cluttered with features. Nearby, the Physick Garden was tended by William Aiton, the head gardener, and a Flower Garden and parterre could also be admired. Amusement was provided by a beautiful and brightly painted Chinese fretwork aviary and a menagerie (figs. 78, 79).

To the south-east, the ground was dotted with temples, some nestling in greenery, others set up on mounds or on open ground where they could be seen from afar. Chambers dabbled in a rather whimsical way with these, initially establishing a few, and then, probably encouraged by Princess Augusta, built yet more, articulated in differing Classical styles and drawing inspiration from ancient ruins. The Temple of Bellona was masculine and Doric, a favourite architectural order of Prince George, adorned with militaristic motifs. Nearby lay temples dedicated to deities such as Pan and Aeolus. The former contin-ued the Doric theme, with ox-skulls in the frieze; here was one of Chambers's earliest attempts, using motifs copied from the Theatre of Marcellus at Rome. The temple doubled as a partially enclosed seat, looking towards a thicket. The Temple of Aeolus, observed by Kielmansegge, was made of timber and was adapted with a revolving seat; it was probably intended to supplant that of Pan. A sudden change of mood was evoked by the House of Confucius, which Chambers had moved to the head of the lake and embellished (fig. 80).

The path then wound its way along the banks of the lake, and on past the site of Merlin's Cave to a semicircular Corinthian colonnade, enclosing another sylvan seat that looked back across the lake and lawn towards the White House. Chambers dedicated this as a Theatre of Augusta, where the Princess could indulge in theatrical parties, and indeed there are accounts that mention canvas awnings and screens erected for the purpose. On a small mound, where the giant flagstaff now stands, was a Temple of Victory in whose design the Prince himself may have had a hand (fig. 66). At this point the path led through the Ruined Arch, carefully contrived to look like a Classical ruin, and evoking a feeling of Roman-tic melancholy (fig. 81). The Romantic overtones were not universally approved of, as one contemporary observer noted that the structure used parliamentary (i.e. contemporary) brick.

The visitor now reached what must have been a

78. A View of the Menagerie
and its Pavilion in the Royal
Gardens at Kew, *after Thomas
Sandby, 1763. The menagerie
consisted of a pond within an
enclosure that had a brightly
painted Chinese pavilion or
'ting' set upon an island.
Around the pond were pens for
rare birds such as Tartarian
pheasants, which today roam
freely in the area around Queen
Charlotte's Cottage.*

79. The Aviary in Kew
Gardens *from the* Universal
Magazine, 1772. *The fretwork
of the large cage was itself
brightly painted. It housed
"barbary pigeons, pheasants,
doves, setting hens and small
birds".*

80. The House of Confucius
*by Charles Edward Papendiek.
William Chambers repositioned
the structure within a grove,
with a covered walkway to an
earlier surviving seat supposedly
devised by William Kent. In
1813, Edward Hawthorn was
paid to apply serpentine strips
and shadows to the roof, to
paint bells and chains in
various colours, and to make
masks in high relief. He used
red, blue, vermilion, Naples
yellow and Chinese green.*

relatively remote part of the garden and encountered the broad vista that took in the three unlikely companions: the surviving pagoda, an Alhambra and a mosque (fig. 82), the last situated on the site of the present Japanese gate. Here Chambers indulged his fantasy as nowhere else, freed from a slavish adherence to better-known Classical architectural principles, and indeed his creations were the subject of criticism by some startled observers, but also started a rash of copies and imitations across Europe.

The pagoda, so closely identified with the modern gardens, broke the skyline and was a sensation of the time. Horace Walpole noted that "we begin to per-ceive the tower of Kew from Montpelier Row; in a fortnight you will be able to see it in Yorkshire", though some time later, having experienced the climb, he was of the opinion that it "yet sees neither London nor the Thames, nor has a room in it". In both senses he was mistaken. Chambers was careful to elucidate the geometry and reasoning behind this 'Chinese taa', of which he was so evidently proud. The ten individual roofs were slated with varnished iron. Count Bentheim observed them in 1784 to be alternating bands of green and white, but this effect lasted just over twenty years before being replaced by common grey slate. The chief glory was the presence

of dragons, eighty in number, attached to the hip of each roof, which are all now lost. They were probably painted with enamels or ground-glass particles over a timber core, to give a dazzling iridescence. Thus, shimmering with colour, the pagoda rose to a gilded stupa, adorned with bells and chains.

Chambers is usually said to have derived his designs for the Alhambra from a drawing by the Swiss painter John Müntz, which had more in common with a Venetian palazzo than anything *mudéjar*, and indeed Walpole was close to the truth when he described it as "ill imagined, and I dare say like the buildings of no country". The design had a salon and portico of coupled columns, adorned with decoration painted to resemble ceramic tiles, and all topped by a viewing pavilion and balustrade, which drew on Greek anthemion motifs, topped with Gothic crocketed pinnacles. The roof was grey, with a red and green frieze around the arches and dark blue facing covered with gold stars. There was also red, yellow ochre and white, while the ceiling inside was based on a Roman vault. The mosque had the appearance of a great Byzantine church transformed into an Islamic building with a low, squat dome, flanked by

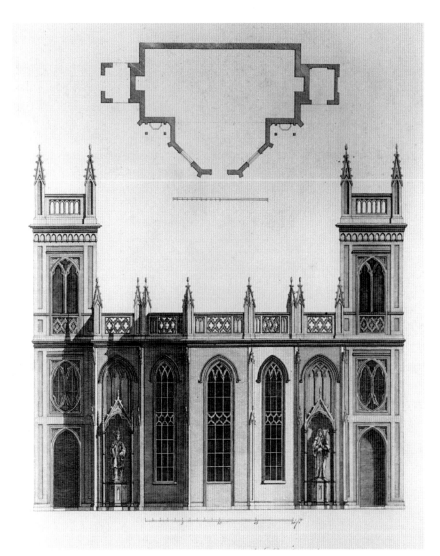

83. *Plan for a Gothic cathedral by John Müntz, c. 1759. The building, erected in a grove in 1759, had been artfully devised in canvas and wood, reaching the level of pure theatricality, and was said to be a riposte by Müntz against the fairytale Gothic of Horace Walpole's house at Strawberry Hill.*

minarets. It was carefully set with a backdrop of bushes and even had a stern and rather curiously critical Arabic admonition inscribed in gold letters around the building, taken from the Koran by Dr Moreton: "Lest there be compulsion in religion, there is not any God beyond God, nor should you set up an image to God." In plan it was like an octagon, with smaller, vaulted chambers flanking it; these were painted rose red, while the main room, lit by arches within, was supported by stuccoed palms, beneath a *trompe-l'œil* sunny sky painted in the dome. Chambers was honest when describing this building. Externally he endeavoured to follow the principles of Turkish architecture, but with the interior "I have not so scrupulously adhered to their style in the buildings, but aimed at something uncommon, and at the same time pleasing". Though a contemporary view enthused that "none of them deserve greater applaude than the beautiful mosque", the building was to last a mere sixteen years before orders were given to take it down and clear it away in 1779.

Having taken in this 'exotic trilogy' the route continued on the east side of Love Lane and passed a Gothic cathedral of canvas and wood (fig. 83). The final encounters on the journey back to the palace would be two rather isolated buildings: the Gallery of Antiques (fig. 84) and the Temple of Solitude. Nothing survives of either building, and still less is known about the rationale behind them. Chambers himself described the whole area at length in a lavishly illustrated tome entitled *Plans, Elevations and Perspective Views at Kew* (1763), dedicated to and indeed paid for by his illustrious patron, the King. "What was once a desart", he exclaimed, "is now an Eden"; a place that covered the deformities of nature and corrected its defects.

There is little doubt that Chambers had his eye on greater things, and indeed the gardens with their picturesque buildings anticipated in their scale the creation of a grand or impressive centrepiece to supplant both Richmond Lodge and the White House. Throughout the first half of the reign, George III dabbled with the idea of constructing a larger palace, of which Chambers would be the natural architect. Kielmansegge noted that he had heard a rumour, as early as 1761, that the King proposed a great new palace, but this may have reflected the first flush of optimism of a new reign and a king eager to express his new authority and taste. A great many designs survive in the Royal Archives for a Palladian, Neo-classical palace by Chambers (figs. 85, 86). This went through several revisions and in 1765 a wooden model was produced, demonstrating the seriousness of the King's intentions, but for a combination of reasons the plans were never put into effect. One scheme was begun opposite Syon, and rose to first-floor level, before being halted and demolished. No

84. The Gallery of Antiques,
*after William Chambers,
c. 1757. The interior of
the gallery, constructed in
1757, was richly carved with
Corinthian columns and was
open to the sky. Niches were
adorned with vases, sphinxes
and statues by Joseph Wilton,
representing the seasons and
the arts.*

trace of it now survives. Chambers was left to express his vision on a much lesser commission at Somerset House, where his masterpiece comes close to the idealized plans. The nearest he got at Kew was a temporary pavilion, erected in canvas and wood close to Richmond Lodge for the reception of the King of Denmark in 1768.

The early 1760s were important from many perspectives. The new reign was represented by a vibrant new monarch who seemed to embrace the Enlightenment and who presided over a country for which military and naval supremacy were assured by a resounding victory over the French in 1763. The Treaty of Paris of that year, ending the Seven Years' War, saw most of the nascent French Empire pass into British hands, paving the way for a second, mercantile British Empire, just as the first rumblings of discontent in America were being felt.

George also stood at the centre of a far-flung European dynastic family that embraced Frederick the Great of Prussia and much of Protestant Europe. Visits by European princes, Queen Charlotte's Mecklenburg relatives and royal gardeners ensured a minor spate of mosques and pagodas in princely gardens across Europe. Kew in the 1760s lay at the epicentre of a very European phenomenon. In the gardens, George III, Princess Augusta, Bute and Chambers created what was at once a reflection of mid-eighteenth-century society and an education, in which Classicism could be used both as an exemplar of architecture and wisdom, and as a series of eye-catching props in an Arcadian landscape. Just as William Kent had begun developing his little buildings at Richmond Gardens, so thirty years later Chambers was quick to expand, but on a far more sumptuous and enduring scale.

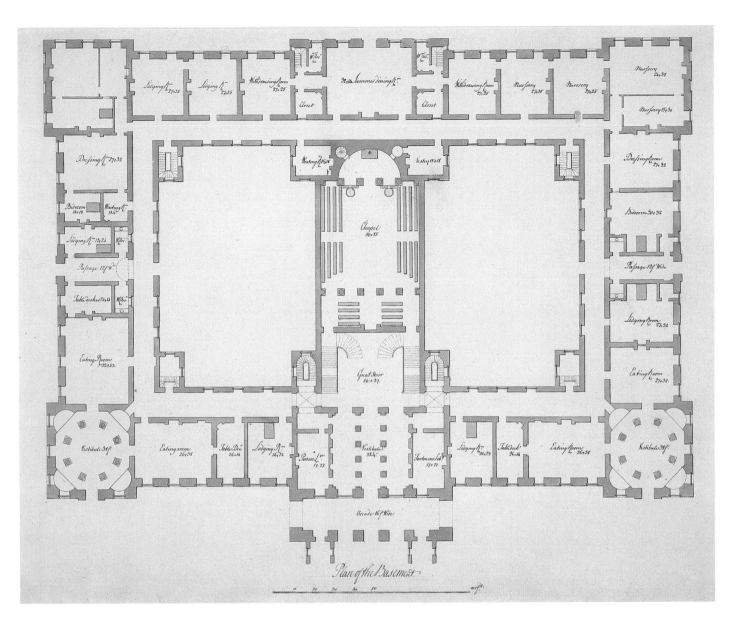

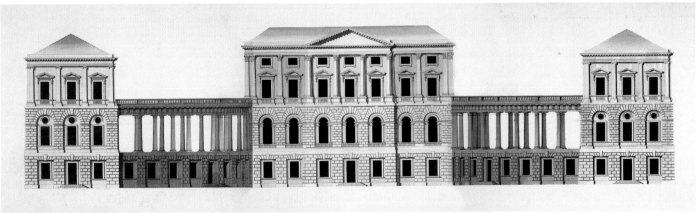

TOP 85. Design for Richmond
Palace *by Sir William
Chambers, 1765. Although
the palace was never built,
many such designs exist,
usually based on Palladian
principles, combining
rustication, colonnades,
grandiose pavilions and
pedimented fronts.*

ABOVE 86. Design for Richmond Palace: Side Elevation *by Sir
William Chambers, c. 1770. Chambers's designs are imaginative,
though always confined within Palladian principles. This example
combined a large central block, raised on two storeys of rusticated
masonry, with flanking pavilions, reached by somewhat impractical
open curved colonnades. The design has echoes of William Kent's
designs for Holkham Hall in Norfolk.*

A *new* GEORGIAN *Reign* 1760–72

During the early days of his reign, the young George III establishes his lifelong interests at Kew, which encompass farming, architecture, natural philosophy, astronomy and family life.

The accession of the new King

On the morning of 25 October 1760, George, Prince of Wales was travelling to London from Kew. He had hardly reached Chiswick when he was met by the King's messenger, who handed him a note that made him turn about immediately. George II had died that morning at Kensington Palace. At twenty-two George was now king.

It was to Lord Bute that George returned at Kew and to him that the new King turned for support, retaining him as his Groom of the Stool and, more disastrously, encouraging him to become Prime Minister, with the result that the King's early reign was blighted with many acrimonious changes of administration. In Cinderella fashion the German principalities had been scoured for a suitable wife for the young George, and shortly before his coronation in October 1761 he married Princess Charlotte of Mecklenburg-Strelitz (fig. 88). The monarchy had passed from an ageing, solitary, foreign figure who valued Hanover above his adopted country to a young married man who declared that he gloried in the name of Britain.

On 12 October the newly-weds went to Richmond to dine. Richmond Lodge had been granted to Charlotte on her marriage and she expressed delight in "the beautiful and charmingly situated palace". It is related that George found the doors of the gardens at Richmond locked to the public and demanded that they should be opened, saying to his gardener, "My subjects, Sir, walk where they please." The gardener complained that the visitors tore up the flowers and shrubs but was told in no uncertain terms that he should plant more. In later years the King would be less tolerant of this public intrusion.

Jeremiah Meyer, who had a house on Kew Green, painted miniature portraits of the royal family. His profile of George III was used on silver shillings and sixpences minted in 1787.

Queen Charlotte wrote to Lady Charlotte Finch in 1771: "I am glad to hear that the children are to spend their time at Kew ... they never can be in better hands than yours."

George III was keenly interested in natural philosophy and had a large collection of instruments. This richly ornamented silver microscope was made for George IV when Prince of Wales and was similar to one owned by George III.

ABOVE 89. Richmond Lodge
by Paul Sandby, c. 1770.
A London guidebook of 1767
commented, "Their present
majesties having made this
palace their chief summer
residence, the apartments are
sumptuously ornamented. The
building is magnificent; and
the park and gardens, which
are kept in extraordinary good
order, are exceedingly pleasant
and well disposed." The two
boys in the foreground are
probably George, Prince of
Wales (later George IV)
and his brother Frederick,
Duke of York.

RIGHT 90. Horace Walpole
observed, "the King loves
medals". George III had
15,000 by the end of his reign.
He kept some of his collection
at Richmond Lodge in medal
cabinets such as this one,
which was made for him
by William Vile in 1755.

The royal family returns to Richmond Lodge

Since Queen Caroline's death in 1737, Richmond
Lodge had been little used, although George II
visited it weekly in his later years. Walpole recorded,
"Every Saturday in summer he carried that uniform
party, but without his daughters, to dine at Richmond. They went in coaches and six in the middle of
the day, with the heavy horseguards kicking up the
dust before them, dined, walked an hour in the
garden, returned in the same dusty parade."

It was not until 1764 that the new King and Queen
went to Richmond Lodge for a prolonged summer
visit. In the meantime, they had acquired a London
residence: Buckingham House, renamed the Queen's
House – and today known as Buckingham Palace.
Charlotte had already given birth to two sons,
George, the new Prince of Wales, and Prince
Frederick, and was pregnant again. A new, larger
summer palace was clearly needed but, for the
moment, the old Richmond Lodge was fitted up for
their reception. The housekeeper Mrs Tunstall
arranged to have the chimneys swept and the
King's new gardener, Mr Haverfield, tidied the
gardens, and clocks, paintings and a harpsichord
were delivered to the lodge. The walls were recovered with a green embossed paper with borders
and, in the Great Room, with Indian paper on a
dark blue background. Mahogany furniture made by

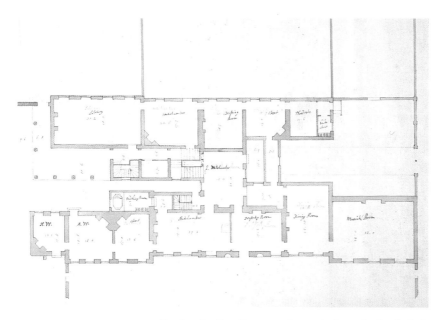

Benjamin Goodison was brought in and a book desk and a case by William Vile in which to house the King's collection of medals (fig. 90). The young Prince of Wales had a bedchamber fitted out in green silk and his brother Prince Frederick had yellow silk curtains to his room. Fine netting was installed over each child's bed – presumably against mosquitoes, although rats, fleas and bedbugs were also common hazards at Richmond and Kew. Finally, the Richmond bellringers were paid two guineas to ring in the royal family on their arrival. They rang again to celebrate the Prince of Wales's second birthday on 12 August. Then both children caught whooping cough and were isolated in the now empty Kew Palace, while Queen Charlotte suffered a miscarriage. In her strolls through the gardens during her convalescence, the teenage Queen may have reflected on the grandmother who had died a few months before her

husband's birth and who had created the strange buildings of Merlin's Cave and the Hermitage in Richmond Gardens, and on her mother-in-law who in the past few years had created a host of outlandish buildings in the gardens next door, including the lofty pagoda now dominating the skyline.

It soon became apparent that Richmond Lodge was too small to accommodate the King and Queen's growing family. Possibly the use of Kew Palace the previous year for the recuperation of the young princes gave rise to the idea of expanding the royal nursery to Kew. The palace nominally belonged to the Duke of York – the King's brother – but he now spent most of his time abroad in poor health and died in Monaco in 1767. The Dowager Princess Augusta returned from Carlton House to her old home, the White House at Kew, for a few hours only each week in summer to breakfast with her eldest son and his family; otherwise Miss Duck, one of the daughters of Stephen Duck the poet, was employed as housekeeper. Other houses at Kew acquired by Queen Caroline in 1728 were available: the Queen's House on the green and the Ferry House and an adjacent house on the river.

A child-care routine soon developed: the newest baby stayed at Richmond Lodge with its parents and after a year, when there was usually a new sibling to take its place, would progress to the houses at Kew where the royal governess, Lady Charlotte Finch, and her assistant Mrs Cotesworth were provided with rooms. As the number of children grew, Lady Charlotte was given her own house with a garden, next door to the Ferry House, which was occupied by Joshua Kirby, Clerk of the Works and Drawing Master to the royal children. Lady Charlotte had been appointed on the birth of the Prince of Wales and

was to become a close friend of the Queen, maintaining an affectionate correspondence with the family to the end of her life. She brought the King and Queen's third son, Prince William (later William IV), to Richmond most Tuesdays and Saturdays, sometimes accompanying the royal family on a walk around the gardens or on a local outing, once to Strawberry Hill, the Gothic house of Horace Walpole, and occasionally to dine with the princes' grandmother Princess Augusta at the White House.

On a Sunday the family often went to the White Lodge in Richmond Park, to avoid the crowds who turned out to visit Richmond Gardens on their public open day. Among the visitors there was often to be found Lady Mary Coke, the daughter of the Duke of Argyll and a local resident at Sudbrook House. She was a friend of Princess Amelia and of Lady Charlotte Finch and often visited her, and consequently the young princes, at Kew. Lady Mary was most enchanted by the four-year-old Prince of Wales, whom she described as "the most comical child I ever saw".

The new King and Queen lived more like country gentry than royalty at Richmond (fig. 102). Horace Walpole complained of the excess of privacy and economy in which they passed their time – the beef required for their soup was restricted to four pounds and they were waited on at dinner by only the Queen's hairdresser. By eighteenth-century standards both the King, who was conscious of his tendency to put on weight, and the Queen were very moderate eaters but they were lampooned for their frugality. They introduced their children to a diet that

we would still consider healthy and in which moderation was again the keynote: plain meat without fat or sauce, days free from meat or fish, plenty of fresh vegetables, fruit without pastry and a choice of one ice only – a diet from which, to his cost, the Prince of Wales was to stray far in later life. There was still fun on royal birthdays, as there had been when the King was a boy at Kew. On his fourth birthday, the Prince of Wales was dressed as a sailor and danced a hornpipe for his parents at Richmond Lodge, while Prince Frederick, the new titular bishop of the German town of Osnabrück, appeared as Harlequin and baby William as "a Mademoiselle". Then there were boat races on the river and a concert in the evening. It was probably in this year that the King saw his now estranged "dearest friend" Lord Bute for the last time in the Dowager Princess's gardens at Kew. The King's emotions had been too engaged with Bute for him to want to be reminded of their former friendship. But Bute had been extremely instrumental in forming the tastes of the young King.

Farmer George

George III took a personal interest in the farming, buildings and management of his estate at Richmond. Botany was for him always a lesser attraction, so while William Aiton was tending the exotic collection at next-door Kew, the King introduced Lancelot 'Capability' Brown as his new royal gardener. Brown soon set about re-landscaping the area around Richmond Lodge, obliterating the nearby hamlet of West Sheen, the river terrace and most of Queen Caroline's

garden buildings in the process, although the Hermitage, in a ruined condition, survived into the nineteenth century. There was much protest: William Mason put his views into verse on "untutor'd Brown" who

> ... rudely rushed and levelled Merlin's Cave:
> Knock'd down the waxen Wizzard, seiz'd his wand
> Transformed to lawn what late was Fairy land;
> And marr'd with impious hand each sweet design
> Of Stephen Duck and good Queen Caroline.

In effect, the flat lands of the Richmond–Kew borders were to give George III the first chance to practise what was to become his lifelong passion – farming.

The Observatory

Events of the time, and the King's own scientific interests, resulted in a short burst of building activity in Richmond Gardens. The impending transit of Venus, whereby the path of the planet is visible as it passes across the face of the sun, had immense significance for the scientific community in the eighteenth century, as it enabled accurate measurements of the distance of the sun and the size of the solar system to be calculated. The first transit cycle in over a hundred years had already occurred in June 1761, but the second, due to take place on 3 June 1769, was eagerly anticipated. The King had helped finance the recording of the transit in the South Pacific being undertaken by Captain Cook on board HMS *Endeavour* with the botanical explorers Joseph Banks, Daniel Solander and Sydney Parkinson. In order for George to view the transit himself, a special observatory was commissioned from William Chambers, paid for by Princess Augusta, which survives in splendid isolation in the Old Deer Park (fig. 95).

The building itself was constructed as an elegant Palladian villa, having a central bay window rising to a principal storey and mezzanine, with flanking lower wings which have since been raised. This was rendered in Chambers's favourite stucco and was surmounted by an enclosing balustrade with a little squat cupola, reached by a narrow circular stair. The building had a double purpose as a virtual temple to astronomy. The main salon, which rose through the two storeys, was fitted up by James Arrow with a fine and delicate staircase and balustrade, and walls lined with glass-fronted cabinets of *chinoiserie* fretwork,

97. Queen Charlotte with Members of her Family *by Johan Zoffany, 1771–72. Queen Charlotte is seen seated with her family in the gardens at Kew. She restrains the ever-boisterous and newly breeched William while, at her knee, the Princess Royal clasps her doll. Lady Charlotte Finch holds baby Ernest. To the left stands the Queen's brother Charles, and to the right her brother Ernest, princes of Mecklenburg-Strelitz.*

for housing the numerous astronomical and mathematical instruments that the King had purchased, along with a collection of ores from his dominions in Germany. Not everybody approved, and it was reported in the *London Magazine* in 1774 that "the observatory is a bauble of extravagance ill placed; it contains a great collection of useless books and instruments".

The Observatory was finished in time for the transit and an excited party gathered around the telescope. It included Queen Charlotte and her two brothers on a visit from Mecklenburg-Strelitz, Benjamin Vulliamy, the King's clockmaker, John Cuff, his instrument-maker, and Stephen Demainbray, whose rôle it was to position George to be the first to view the transit.

The exotic and the picturesque

By a long-established tradition, the royal family received gifts of exotic animals and specimens brought from distant lands and presented to the monarch. Collecting was considered an important royal pastime and little menageries were scattered across several royal properties. The early Hanoverians kept cages and enclosures for tortoises and wild cats at Kensington Palace, and Queen Charlotte had a zebra and an elephant in the gardens at the Queen's House in London. Queen Caroline's tigers had long since gone from Richmond, but Queen Charlotte kept an elk and a mouse-coloured

deer, which may have been housed in a row of pens and a paddock that appear on contemporary plans to the north of Richmond Lodge, among Bridgeman's serpentine wooded walks. There may also have been an aviary on the site, as well as a cottage for the keeper.

Queen Charlotte's Cottage

Capability Brown's notions of a romantic, unplanned landscape had begun to sweep across the area in the later eighteenth century, with more naturalistic layouts populated by wistful ruins and artisans' cottages. The *cottage orné*, or picturesque building, was one expression of this, sometimes used as a home for estate workers and at other times functioning as a tea-house or pavilion. By 1771, just such a building had appeared on the site of the earlier menagerie. Queen Charlotte's Cottage, as it became known, ranks as an important early example of its kind. Moreover, it is the only building that reflects the tastes and interests of the Queen herself (fig. 98).

The building falls into two distinct parts, and was given a carefully contrived rustication by using seventeenth-century window frames with quaint, old-fashioned leaded panes, poor-quality 'place' bricks, normally never seen on facing masonry, and a thatched roof of reed and rye straw. There are several incongruities suggesting that the effect has

RIGHT 98. *Queen Charlotte's Cottage. The central two-storey bay of brick comprises two large chambers, one set above the other, with small projecting porches to two entrances – one for servants and the other for the royal family. This is repeated to the rear so that, with the flanking stairs, the building has absolute symmetry. It was used by the royal family to take tea and have picnics.*

BELOW 99. *Queen Charlotte's Cottage, after George Ernest Papendiek, published 1820. Papendiek's flowing lines make the building look more ramshackle than it really is, but the cottage has changed little since this view was made. It was designed to look picturesque and continues to draw visitors to its relative peace and isolation in the gardens.*

been taken too far. The exposed timber of the stair turrets is almost vulgar in its effect, with slender framing of softwood – displaying indiscriminate carpentry marks, such as would only be seen on an internal stud wall – which would never have endured a wet climate. It is feasible that the effect was meant to replicate the narrow timber-framing with which Queen Charlotte would have been familiar on farms in her native Mecklenburg, but it is more likely that the turrets and upper parts of the building were originally rendered and painted. The earliest view, of about 1820, shows that the cottage had been stripped, perhaps to enhance its sylvan appearance (fig. 99). Other frivolous touches include the nonsense of its rusticated doors, battened at odd angles, with their supporting ledges to the exterior instead of inside, where they belong.

Though the cottage must have presented a perfect picture, set within its glade, with wisps of smoke drifting gently from the chimney, internally there is nothing rustic about the building. The elegant staircases are set over a splendid geometrical stone floor, while the walls are bevelled and the quality of the craftsmanship is the finest. The lower room was hung with prints by Hogarth (fig. 100). Tea could be taken in the well-proportioned upper chamber with its fine views and unusual parabolic roof, later (around 1804) decorated with a painted trellis by George and Charlotte's third daughter, Princess Elizabeth (figs. 101, 133).

The cottage was a place of diversion for the royal family. It has such architectural subtlety that its design must have come from a practised hand. Chambers has often been credited with the cottage, which displays the modesty of the family, in contrast to the self-indulgent Petit Trianon at Versailles, which is usually held up as the epitome of the *cottage orné*. Kew anticipated these trends by a number of years.

100. *The Print Room in Queen Charlotte's Cottage. The prints were almost exclusively by Hogarth and attached by brackets rather than pasted on to the wall as was normally the fashion. The idea for a print room may have been inspired by a similar contemporary room at nearby Syon House.*

Richmond Gardens become a fashionable promenade

At the end of the first decade of the reign of George III, the gardens at Richmond veered between exclusive royal use and a select tourist attraction as ever greater numbers clamoured for access on Sundays. Lady Mary Coke moved between both private and public circles. On a very hot day in July 1769 she dined with Lady Charlotte Finch at Kew and saw the young princes dance. She was also shown the little four-wheeled carriage drawn by a small white pony. The princes were very pleased with it, especially as they were allowed to travel in it by themselves through the gardens from the nursery at Kew as far as Richmond Lodge with only a page hanging on to their coat-tails to stop them falling out. A very different experience was had by the visitors who came to the gardens on a Sunday evening. They caused huge traffic jams in the area, some even finding it difficult to leave "due to the great quantity of equipages on Kew Green".

One Sunday a sudden rainstorm elicited the following anecdote from Lady Mary Coke:

The distress of the very numerous and brilliant company in Richmond Gardens on Sunday evening occasioned by the sudden and long continued heavy rain was beyond description. Beaux and belles of all ranks and degrees were all but drowned ... . Some were bewildered and kept so late in the gardens that they could not get out in time and were confined there, wet to the skin and all night while their carriages waited for them in vain without ... . The Prince of Mecklenburgh, the Spanish ambassador and his lady with many persons of rank and distinction shared in the general misfortune. The inns at Richmond, Kew were so crowded that ten guineas was refused for a bed and several persons of condition were obliged to lie all night upon straw.

101. The Picnic Room at Queen Charlotte's Cottage. The parabolic roof adds an unusual touch and was later embellished with a painted trellis by Princess Elizabeth (see fig. 133).

GEORGE III *and* *Queen* Charlotte at KEW 1772–88

The 1770s are a golden decade at Kew for the royal family, "a scene beyond Elysium blest".
However, the next decade brings misfortune that will overshadow the remainder of the reign.

102. Their Majesties walking in Kew-Gardens, 1787. Many commented on the royal couple's informality and lack of attendants at Kew but, like his father, Frederick, George III took little care for his personal safety. The King and Queen drove unescorted through the streets of Richmond; on one such occasion, it was reported, the Queen had a shoe thrown at her.

103. William Chambers's clock tower, after George Ernest Papendiek, published 1820. The tower, which stood to the east of the White House, may have been among the few proposed alterations that were actually carried out by William Chambers for George III. The clock mechanism was made by John Smith, who installed it in 1777 under the watchful and interested eye of the King. In the mid-nineteenth century the mechanism was removed and reused by Queen Victoria at Osborne House. The tower was probably demolished in the 1850s.

From Richmond to Kew

The King's mother, the Dowager Princess Augusta, died at Carlton House in London in February 1772. A few weeks later Queen Charlotte wrote to her brother Charles, "We are exchanging Richmond for Kew this summer." George III with his family returned to his boyhood home of the White House. Without either ceremony or apparent nostalgia, Richmond Lodge was finally abandoned and a few months later demolished. Plans were certainly drawn up to remodel and enlarge the White House, but the lack of both documentary evidence and archaeological remains have thrown doubt upon whether any modifications were ever undertaken. William Chambers may have enlarged some of the buildings around the stable block and he did create a pretty clock tower, surmounted by a cupola with a bell (figs. 103, 105).

Two estates united

With the family home, the White House, George III now inherited the 300 acres of the two estates of Richmond and Kew, bordered by the Kew road to the east and the River Thames to the west, from Kew Palace in the north to the Observatory in the south. There was agricultural land in plenty, kitchen and flower gardens, the new cottage and, at the heart of it all, Augusta's and Bute's great pleasure grounds, sprinkled with Chambers's garden buildings.

Joseph Banks (1743–1820), the botanist and explorer, became a frequent visitor to the King at Kew, bringing with him on one occasion in 1774 the newly arrived Tahitian warrior Omai (fig. 106). Banks was to become a close friend of the King. George III, who in his whole life never travelled further than a hundred or so miles from the capital, was fascinated by Banks's tales of adventure and curious to see the plans of his voyages. Banks also brought from the South Seas a collection of over a thousand new seeds and plants, which Mr Aiton duly planted and labelled in the botanic garden at Kew (fig. 108). Under Banks's direction, the botanic garden was put on a more scientific footing and Aiton began compiling a catalogue of the plants being introduced, the celebrated *Hortus Kewensis* (1789), still continued today. Although the paling separating the old Richmond and Kew gardens had long since been

Joseph Banks was knighted in 1781. During the ceremony, George III whispered to him, "Sir Jos: I have many years wishd to do this."

In July 1776, Joseph Wilton's gilded lead statue of George III in New York was pulled down by American patriots. The metal was used to make over 80,000 bullets to fire on the King's troops.

In 1786, a mentally deranged woman, Margaret Nicholson, tried to assassinate George III outside St James's Palace. The King calmly said: "The poor creature is mad. Do not hurt her. She has not hurt me."

104. Proposals for alterations to the White House, *William Chambers, c. 1772. With plans for a large, new palace in Richmond Gardens abandoned, Chambers drew up a scheme to enlarge the White House with a grander north façade and proposed remodelling the centre of the house. There is, however, no archaeological or documentary evidence that this work was ever carried out.*

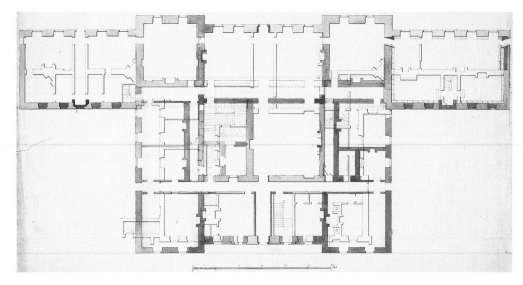

105. View of Kew Gardens *by John Fisher, Bishop of Salisbury, c. 1800. Fisher was a friend and patron of the artist John Constable, and an amateur painter himself. His view of the White House reveals the well-developed landscape surrounding the house and the beautiful setting of the building. Chambers's clock tower can be seen to the right.*

106. Omiah, the Indian from Otaheite presented to their Majesties at Kew by Mr Banks & Dr Solander, July 17 1774. *Three days after Omai arrived from Tahiti, Banks and Solander took him to meet the King and Queen at the White House at Kew. Seen as the epitome of the noble savage, he was painted by Sir Joshua Reynolds. He was the toast of London for a couple of years before he returned to Tahiti in 1777.*

PLAN
of the Royal Manor of
RICHMOND
otherwise
WEST SHEEN,
in the County of Surry,
a GRANT to
HER MAJESTY.
Taken under the Direction of
PETER BURRELL Esq.
His Majesty's Surv.r Gen.l
in 1771. by Tho.s Richardson in
York Street Covendish Square

ABOVE 107. Plan of the Royal
Manor of Richmond *by
Thomas Richardson, 1771.
This beautifully executed map
shows the varied nature of the
landscape around Richmond
and Kew. The formally defined
lawns and lakes of Kew Gardens
contrast with the more heavily
wooded and naturalistic
landscape of Richmond
Gardens, to the west. The
ancient strip-fields around
Richmond were still clearly
defined at this date.*

RIGHT 108. *Sir James Everard
Home presented to Kew the*
Fuchsia coccinea, *from South
America, in 1788. Sir Joseph
Banks carried the original
fuchsia into the garden on his
head, choosing not to trust it
to any other person.*

FUCHSIA coccinea

taken down, it was not until 1785 that legislation was passed enabling Love Lane to be closed to the public and, still later, in 1802, that the boundary walls between the two estates were finally removed.

The upbringing of the royal children

On the eighth birthday of the Prince of Wales, Queen Charlotte had sent him a pocket book with a letter outlining her "wishes concerning your future conduct in life" and telling him that "the time draws near when you will be put into the hands of governors". That time had come. The Prince of Wales and Prince Frederick moved into Kew Palace with their own household and governor, Lord Holderness, Preceptor, Dr Markham, and Leonard Smelt. It was the same house in which George III had received his own education. He had been the eldest son of eight children born to Frederick before his early death; now, living in Frederick's family house at Kew, the King likewise had eight children, the eldest of whom he too had

109. Mary Granville, Mrs Delany *by Joseph Brown after John Opie, 1891. The royal family occasionally visited Bulstrode, the home of Lady Portland, with whom Mrs Delany lived; they became increasingly fond of her. Queen Charlotte sent her flower specimens from Kew from which she created "paper mosaicks" with "precision and truth unparalleled". George III invited Mrs Delany to stay at Kew and later gave her a house at Windsor.*

110. *Lady Charlotte Finch, the royal governess, gave daily lessons to the young princes and princesses using 'educational toys', such as jigsaws, which she designed herself, and possibly these nursery counters to teach letters and words. The Prince of Wales, whose emblem of three feathers is shown on the lid of the container, was a precocious child and learnt without difficulty.*

The King and Queen took a detailed interest in their children's education and upbringing when they were at Kew, which was the only place where they could indulge in anything approaching a normal domestic family life. Brought from their respective houses, the children breakfasted with their parents and, if there were no lessons, took an airing in the gardens, sometimes in the company of their mother and father. The elder princes learnt about farming and in the garden behind Kew Palace reportedly grew a small patch of wheat from seed, then harvested and threshed it to produce the flour to bake a loaf of bread for the royal table. More regular lessons included mathematics, history, natural philosophy and literature, and the polite arts of fencing, music and drawing.

The princesses occasionally took a share in the princes' activities and the young Princess Augusta enjoyed a game of cricket or football with her brothers. Like all children they enjoyed boisterous play – poor Uncle Ernest ended up with a black eye from a bout of their rough games.

The princesses' formal education was less rigid than that of their brothers and they were allowed more artistic pursuits, with the occasional magic lantern show for fun. Lady Charlotte Finch was an inventive teacher and history lessons were brightened by the use of picture cards and geography lessons by the use of some of the first jigsaws (fig. 110).

Mrs Papendiek, daughter of Mr Albert, the Queen's hairdresser, lived at Kew during this period and described these golden days when the elder children were young:

> Kew now became quite gay, the public being admitted to the Richmond Gardens on Sundays, and to Kew Gardens on Thursdays. The Green on those days was covered with carriages, more than £300 being often taken at the bridge on Sundays. Their Majesties were to be seen at the windows speaking to their friends, and the royal children amusing themselves, in their own gardens. Parties came up by water too, with bands of music, to the ait [island] opposite the Dutch House. The whole was a scene of enchantment and delight; Royalty living amongst their subjects to give pleasure and to do good.

Changing times

In the summer of 1776, the King discovered the good hunting and farming potential of Windsor. A house to the south of the castle, which had belonged to Queen Anne (1702–14), was rebuilt by Chambers and became known as the Upper or the Queen's Lodge. Across the gardens, the Lower Lodge was built for the accommodation of the royal children, particularly the princesses. Given the need to attend St James's Palace each week for court ceremonial, an additional country

christened George. Kew, as at so many times during its royal history, was full of echoes, but in 1772 there was too much happening in the present to allow time for reminiscing.

The Prince of Wales and Prince Frederick went weekly to dine with their governor and his family at Syon Hill. They were now also invited to the occasional royal birthday or celebration Drawing Room (a formal court assembly) at St James's Palace, where, in 1772, the ten-year-old Prince of Wales told Lady Mary Coke "he had a great deal of conversation with the Foreign Ministers". Every summer the royal children were invited to visit their great-aunt Amelia's fine Palladian villa at nearby Gunnersbury. They arrived in great state, dined and then embarked on a series of riotous games, including Goose (a board game) and skittles. This was followed by card and chance games such as commerce and shilling loo. On one occasion a band played especially for two-year-old Ernest, who amused all the company with his dancing.

residence caused travelling problems. The Queen became stressed with the difficulty of meeting up with the children, to whom she often referred at this time as her "*bande joyeuse*". Soon Sunday, Monday and Tuesday would be spent at Windsor, Wednesday and Thursday had to be London days and it was only on Friday and Saturday that the Queen saw her children at Kew. Yet still more children piled into the royal nursery: Augustus in 1773, Adolphus in 1774, Mary in 1776 and Sophia in 1777.

As the babies continued to arrive, the elder princes entered adolescence. Lord Holderness, described by Walpole as "that formal piece of dullness", despaired of a schoolhouse of insubordination at Kew Palace and resigned. Holderness, Markham and Smelt were replaced with an initially stricter régime under the Duke of Montagu, with Dr Richard Hurd as Preceptor and George Hotham. The Prince of Wales was now sixteen and his own teenage rebellion was just beginning as the King travelled to Portsmouth to review the Royal Navy setting to sea to confront the rebellious colonies in far-away America.

The idyll ends

The golden days of the 1770s were ending, but one more gem was to be discovered. In February 1779 was born the thirteenth child and eighth son, Prince Octavius, who seemed to charm all those who came into contact with him (fig. 111). During the same year, the Prince of Wales fell in love with Mary Hamilton, the princesses' young attendant. Then he more dangerously transferred his passions to the actress Mary 'Perdita' Robinson, with secret late-night assignations at Kew (fig. 113). The young Prince was out of his depth and the affair ended badly, with Perdita returning the Prince's adolescent love letters to the King in return for £5000. Prince William, aged fourteen, left his house on Kew Green for life as a midshipman in the Royal Navy. At Kew, Chambers's Turkish mosque fell into disrepair and was cleared away; a little tea-house sprang up near Queen Charlotte's Cottage with a painted cloth roof. When in London, the King would sometimes ride over to Kew very early in the morning before his gruelling day at St James's for a quiet half-hour with his children. In September 1780, Alfred was born. Unlike all the previous sturdy children, he was a sickly infant. Prince Frederick departed for military

114. The Eldest Princesses:
Charlotte, Princess Royal,
Augusta and Elizabeth *by
Thomas Gainsborough,
1793–94. As their older
brothers launched themselves
into hedonistic pursuits, the
three older princesses were kept
within strict bounds in London,
Windsor and Kew. Although
denied the chance to meet
eligible princes, they benefited
from a more thorough education
than their younger sisters would
receive. This portrait was
painted for the princesses'
brother George, Prince of
Wales.*

training in Hanover, leaving both King and Prince of Wales distraught, but more grief was in store, for in August 1782 little Alfred died. King George was heard to comment: "I am very sorry for Alfred, but had it been Octavius, I should have died too."

Thomas Gainsborough began his celebrated series of portraits of the royal family, painting Alfred from memory and leaving out Frederick who was in Hanover. The artist described himself as "all but raving mad with ecstasy in beholding such a constellation of youthful beauty". But on a day in early May of 1783 the darling of the family, Octavius, aged four, died at Kew, a few days after his inoculation for smallpox. The King appeared to suffer from this blow more than anyone else, lamenting, "there will be no Heaven for me if Octavius is not there". The last child was born to George and Charlotte in August that year. Princess Amelia was a child most cherished, especially by the still grieving King.

Growing up

The elder children were by now almost grown up. The Princess Royal and Princess Augusta had been introduced at court and had their own lady-in-

waiting. The Prince of Wales had come of age and been granted Carlton House in London (fig. 112). Although he retained Kew Palace, it was hardly to his developing taste and he visited only when required to; the house once again fell quiet. The older princesses (fig. 114) sometimes drove over from London to walk in the grounds at Kew, but the younger princesses when not at the Queen's House spent their days in the new nursery, the Lower Lodge at Windsor. Drawing Rooms at St James's Palace were now fortnightly, which meant that, in the travelling schedule between Windsor and London, Kew had only a scant look-in.

The younger princes began to leave the nest too. Edward, following in the footsteps of his older brother, went for military training in Hanover and the three younger princes went to university in Göttingen, under the tutelage of Professor Lichtenberg, a friend and early visitor to George and Charlotte at Kew. Prince William's travels at sea took him to the West Indies and eventually to the front line in America. He would have preferred a sojourn in the Mediterranean, but as he wrote to the Prince of Wales of their father, "we are both sure old square

toes will not approve of my going there". He added, "I understand the old boy is exceedingly out of humour and I am in hourly expectation of a thunderstorm from that quarter. Fatherly admonitions at our time of life are very unpleasant and of no use." Certainly they had little effect on the Prince of Wales who, kept unemployed at home, had secretly and illegally married a Roman Catholic widow, Maria Fitzherbert. Princess Elizabeth, suffering supposedly from scrofula (tuberculosis of the lymphatic glands), spent many months quietly engaged in artistic and botanic pastimes at Kew.

"The simplest country gentlefolk"
In 1786, Fanny Burney, novelist and diarist, joined the Queen's household as Assistant Mistress of the Robes. Early in her service, the royal family passed some time at Kew. She described the Kew life as very different from that at Windsor:

As there are no early prayers the Queen rises later; and there is no form of ceremony here of any sort, her dress is plain and the hour for the second toilette extremely uncertain. The Royal

family are here always in so very retired a way, that they live as the simplest country gentlefolk. The King has not even an equerry with him, nor the Queen any lady to attend her when she goes her airings.

The following month, a deranged woman named Margaret Nicholson made an attempt on the King's life as he received petitions from the public at St James's Palace. Fanny was again there to record the royal arrival at Kew after this disturbing event:

Kew Green was quite filled with all the inhabitants of the place – the lame, old, blind, sick and infants, who all assembled, dressed in their Sunday garb, to line the sides of the roads through which their Majesties passed, attended by the band of musicians, arranged in the front, who began "God Save the King" the moment they came upon the Green and finished it with loud huzzas.

The Queen, in speaking of it afterwards, said, "I shall always love little Kew for this!"

THE Shadow of 'Madness' 1788–1818

During the 1780s many of George III's ideas for Kew come to fruition but family life is blighted by the King's mysterious illness. The young princes often disappoint the King while the princesses languish at home.

116. George III during his last illness, *attributed to Joseph Lee, c. 1820. Unrecognizable, the King suffered eight years of solitude at Windsor, blind, increasingly deaf and mostly unable to comprehend what was going on around him. He died on 29 January 1820 in the sixtieth year of his reign.*

117. *In this short letter sent in 1788, George III praises the diligence of his son Augustus, who was studying at the University of Göttingen with his younger brother Adolphus ("Dolly"). The second part of the letter refers to the King's bilious attack – the first indication of the porphyria that was to follow in the winter of 1788–89. He describes trying to remove it with "smart discipline", which probably consisted of a rigorous diet. When that failed he went to take the waters at Cheltenham, which similarly provided no cure.*

The King's illness

The first intimation of the illness that was to blight the second half of his reign came in a short letter the King wrote on 17 June 1788 from Kew to his son Augustus in Göttingen when he complained of a bilious attack (fig. 117). By November, his physical symptoms were accompanied by mental derangement. Given the lack of privacy at Windsor, it was decided to move the King to the White House at Kew, where the housekeeper had been told to keep every room aired for occupation at a moment's notice. The doctors decided the Queen and princesses should travel to Kew first, enticing the King to follow. The Queen was already profoundly disturbed at the progress of the King's illness and the lack of consistent medical diagnosis. The time spent from late November 1788 to March 1789 at the White House during the course of the King's illness was his longest visit to Kew in his entire reign.

The Prince of Wales had ordered the allocation of the accommodation at the White House. The King was given the ground-floor rooms fronting the gardens, where a bed and water closet had been installed, with a wing for his doctors and equerries. The rooms over the King's apartments were kept locked up and unoccupied, so that nobody could disturb or overhear him. The Queen took the other rooms on the first floor, sharing a bedchamber with Princess Augusta, with an *ad hoc* dressing room, drawing room and a gallery where she ate, with two princesses' bedchambers beyond. On the second floor were bedchambers for ladies, surgeons and equerries with rooms "like little cells of a convent"

for the maids off a long dark passage. Kew Palace was also furnished and brought into use, housing the Groom of the King's Bedchamber, who was to receive all enquiries relating to the King's health, and providing overflow accommodation as required.

As the Queen was "much displeased with the physicians" so also was the King, who had been lured to Kew on the pretext of being reunited with his family and then locked away from them. The King understandably, but mistakenly, put some of the blame for this on the Queen. The Duke of York wrote to his

Kew June 17th 1788.

My Dear Augustus, I am really happy in writing to you when I can express my approbation of the diligence you have shewn in all your studies for the last three months, I am certain that this will stimulate a continuance of so proper an exertion. I have had a bilious attack but by smart discipline I trust it is quite removed. I should have written this day to Colonel Malortie but am not quite equal to more this post than a few lines to my friend Dolly, Believe me ever

My Dear Augustus

Your most Affectionate Father

George R.

By 1800, Britain suffered an acute shortage of small change, forcing enterprising merchants and traders to coin their own unofficial penny and halfpenny tokens. These often showed local landmarks, such as the White House.

Medals, headbands, belts and fans were produced to mark the recovery of the King in April 1789. This fan made by Princess Elizabeth bears the words "Health restored to one, and happiness to millions".

Cut-out silhouettes were a popular eighteenth-century pastime. The Princess Royal and Princess Elizabeth were both artistic and adept at this skill.

118. A medal depicting Dr Francis Willis. Dr Willis had been a clergyman before becoming a doctor. George III told him, "You have quitted a profession I have always loved and embraced one I most heartily detest." This medal was struck to commemorate the recovery of the King in 1789. The reverse side reads: "Britons Rejoice your King's restored, 1789".

BELOW LEFT 119. A scene from the 1991 play The Madness of George III with Nigel Hawthorne as George III and Harold Innocent as Sir George Baker, the King's regular but most timid physician. Baker was baffled by the King's symptoms and prescribed the Cheltenham waters, physick, laudanum and senna – for which the King "reprimanded him with great displeasure". In late December 1788, at the height of the King's illness, Baker was called to account for having written the word "better" in the official bulletin. It is recorded, "He [Baker] made a regular apology, pleading his age and infirmities and that since the Queen had been angry with him he was frightened."

BELOW RIGHT 120. Fanny Burney by her cousin Edward Francisco Burney, c. 1778. Fanny had just become known through her popular novel Evelina, which drew an invitation from the Queen to join her household as Assistant Mistress of the Robes, a role for which she was not overly suited, sometimes scribbling novels and a diary when she should have been in royal attendance.

brother Augustus on 3 December describing their father's affliction as "a total loss of all rationality". It was as madness that the eighteenth-century physicians understood the illness of George III – today it has been more accurately diagnosed as the metabolic disorder of acute intermittent porphyria. On 5 December, Dr Willis, the 'mad' doctor, arrived at Kew (fig. 118). The King commented to his page that as Dr Willis was now come he could "never more shew his face again in this country and that he would leave it for ever and retire to Hanover". Interspersed with periods of mental derangement over which he had no control were times of lucidity when the King was acutely aware of his condition. Treatment had so far included little more than blistering and the administration of emetics and purgatives. Dr Willis's régime involved the use of a restraining straitjacket or 'waistcoat' and the presence of his own men only about the King (fig. 119). Medical bulletins were required for Parliament, but continually disputed by factions within the King's medical fraternity. On the

bulletins hung the thorny issues of whether and when a regency would need to be declared.

A slow recovery and new distractions

In the New Year, the King's condition began slowly to improve and the Queen and princesses started to pay short evening visits to him in his apartments. Apart from his doctors and Dr Willis's men, the King had seen or been seen by no one. When, however, Dr Willis met Sir Joseph Banks at the Richmond farm, he arranged for the King to encounter him on his daily convalescent walk as if by chance. After that they walked regularly together in Kew Gardens.

A chance remark by the King's equerry had led to a new responsibility for Banks at Kew. The King had been struck by a comparison of his flock of Wiltshire sheep at Richmond Gardens with Spanish sheep that had been imported into Saxony, and the subsequent wool improvement. Banks had acquired some knowledge of merino sheep and the King, who now desired a merino flock of his own, declared him "just the man" for such an enterprise. During their walks, conversation included new ideas for farming, made feasible by industrial progress, and discoveries from voyages introducing new plants, the economic value of which was of great interest to both men. Banks's vision of a botanic garden was far removed from Bute's ideas of a botanic collection and the King's interest in the new ideas was becoming increasingly engaged.

The royal recovery continued to be slow and erratic, giving the Prince of Wales and his friends in the parliamentary opposition occasional reason for hope and the government cause for despair. On one of his January walks in the gardens, the King lay on the grass and refused to get up when the pagoda was not opened for him and he had to be carried back to the house; but by February he was discussing with interest the exotics in the hothouses. When Mr Aiton promised to prepare a basket of exotic plants for Dr

121. *This engraving by William Woollett shows the King's English sheep at Kew. Towards 1790 he acquired from Spain a flock of merino sheep, renowned for the quality of their wool. In August 1804, an auction of part of this Spanish flock was organized by Sir Joseph Banks and took place in pouring rain in the field in front of the pagoda. Captain McArthur, who subsequently exported the sheep to Australia, was a major purchaser at this sale.*

122. The Reconciliation, 1804, by James Gillray. *The Prince of Wales had attempted to bring in a regency during the King's first bout of illness in 1788–89. During the next recurrence in 1801, the Prince gained admittance to the King's presence only on his recovery. The reunion following the 1804 malady was delayed by the Prince until the King's return from Weymouth. Relations between the King and the Prince were at their lowest ebb during this period and these emotional reconciliations were of short duration.*

Willis, the King proposed that he should prepare "another basket, pack up the doctor in it, and send him off at the same time". On 2 February, Fanny Burney found herself out of bounds in the part of the gardens where the King was walking (fig. 120). Upon seeing him advancing towards her she sped off in the opposite direction until ordered to stop, and then experienced a kiss from the King, his hoarse rendition of a Handel oratorio and a rather strange conversation, in which he repeatedly assured her "I am your friend". By contrast, the King visited his Observatory and talked on scientific matters "with the utmost perspicacity" with his astronomer,

Stephen Demainbray. He sent from the White House to Richmond for the local delicacy, 'Maids of Honour' tarts, which he shared out. He acted out scenes from *The Merchant of Venice* and read, appropriately or not, *King Lear*. The Queen had sent for her harpsichord, there being no band allowed, and the King played again on his flute, which he had long since left off. He amused himself with cards, for which he had formerly little taste, and learnt piquet which he played with the Queen, while Princess Augusta read to him from the *Life of Handel*. Little Princess Amelia also now came on the visits and Willis expressed delight in hearing again the King's

LEFT 123. *Greeting card sent from Joseph Banks to Princess Elizabeth, 30 March 1814. The card was painted by Franz Bauer, a botanical artist at Kew who also gave drawing lessons to the Queen and the princesses. Strelitzia reginae, named after the Queen, is shown in the top left-hand corner, while Banksia serrata, a native Australian plant, shown at bottom right, was named after Banks.*

CENTRE 124. A Kangaroo *by George Stubbs, 1771–72. Kangaroos and wallabies were seen by Englishmen for the first time in July 1770 when Captain Cook's* Endeavour *landed on the coast of North Queensland on the newly discovered continent of Australia. Sydney Parkinson, who died on the return journey with about one third of the ship's crew, made a drawing of kangaroos, which was used by George Stubbs to make this painting. Stubbs also used a kangaroo skull that Joseph Banks had brought back.*

RIGHT 125. *Queen Charlotte in 1796 by William Grimaldi, 1801, after Sir William Beechey. The Queen was traumatized by the King's illness of 1788 and fearful of a recurrence. She never fully recovered her spirits or the gaiety shown in the earlier Gainsborough portraits of her. Her hair turned white during this period and she lost a great deal of weight. Her lap dog, Badine, was a constant companion.*

usual singular expression, "What! What! What!" – a sure sign of recovery.

In all this time, the King had not seen the Prince of Wales until a meeting was arranged at Kew on 23 February, when there was a partial reconciliation and the shedding of tears (fig. 122). On 7 March, the two remaining Willis men left Kew and on the 10th the King drove to Westminster to deliver a speech. A regency had been avoided by a whisker.

The exotic gardens

While the Bastille fell and France erupted in revolution in 1789, all was peaceful in the gardens at Kew, where new plants were arriving almost monthly: the first hydrangea, the peony and magnolia from China and plants from the well-named Botany Bay. Under the patronage of Sir Joseph Banks, Franz Bauer became resident artist at Kew and soon became a great favourite with the Queen and princesses, to whom he taught botanical drawing (fig. 123). The oval of pens at Queen Charlotte's Cottage had sheltered colourful pheasants. Subsequently an adjacent three-acre paddock housed docile rare animals, such as buffaloes, which were regularly presented to the royal family. More exotic animals arrived. Kangaroos came to Kew in 1792 with Vice-Admiral Arthur Phillip, the first governor of New South Wales. Banks had first seen, and then eaten, kangaroos in July 1770 on the coast of Queensland and had returned with the skull and skin of this curious "80-lb mouse", from which George Stubbs made a painting (fig. 124). By 1794, the kangaroos were breeding, their numerous offspring offered to unenthusiastic courtiers.

Family diversions

The King made a full recovery and resumed his life of weekends at Windsor and levées on Wednesdays and Fridays in London, with Kew the midweek stopover residence. The Queen accompanied the King, with the three older princesses always in attendance,

RIGHT 126. *Samples of English silk fabric used to make court dresses for Queen Charlotte and the princesses. Silver and gold thread were added for special occasions such as the King's and Queen's birthday celebrations. The card, dated January 1795, shows fabrics used for making wedding clothes for the marriage of George, Prince of Wales to Caroline of Brunswick at the Chapel Royal, St James's Palace.*

FAR RIGHT 127. *James Wyatt (1746–1813) by Charles Turner, after Matthew Cotes Wyatt, published 1829. After visiting his Pantheon in Oxford Street, Horace Walpole wrote to Wyatt that "no man with such talents as yours wants to be distinguished by the Lustre of others". Wyatt was indeed a phenomenon, at ease with both Gothic and Classical designs. Even before he began work on George III's Gothic Castellated Palace at Kew he had transformed Frogmore House at Windsor in a very Classical manner for Queen Charlotte.*

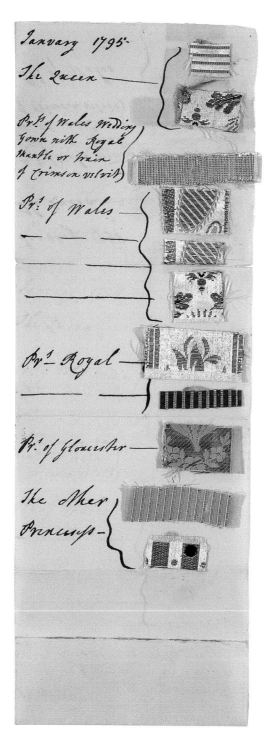

Prince William, returned from sea, set up house at Richmond with the actress Dorothy Jordan and the ten children that they eventually had. Just across the river, another 'unsuitable' neighbour, Maria Fitzherbert, the Prince of Wales's secret and now estranged wife, rented Marble Hill House. Kew Palace meanwhile was again stripped of furniture; the Prince of Wales would use it no more. Lured on with the promise of having his debts paid off, the Prince had married his cousin, Caroline of Brunswick – a disastrous choice (fig. 126).

By January 1797, the Queen, exhausted with moving between three different homes, wrote to the King: "From Monday to Saturday we live in a constant bustle either upon the road or in public; I may now begin to feel the consequences of that life." Fatigue emanated perhaps more from the scandals involving the Prince and Princess of Wales now circulating in the newspapers than from travelling. The King seemed to feel no such fatigue. He added to the estate at Kew, purchasing a house with a large garden on the Green, and met the fashionable architect James Wyatt (1746–1813) to discuss a project that had preoccupied royalty throughout the eighteenth century: the building of a new palace at Kew.

The Castellated Palace

At this time, the fourth and greatest of the royal residences at Kew was conceived, perhaps in the mind of a King under strain from his distressing illness and in the grip of building mania. It was to be a vast edifice, recalling the scale and splendour of the abortive new palaces in Richmond Gardens with which the King had toyed for most of his reign. The architect was to be James Wyatt (fig. 127) and the style, most unusually for the Crown, Gothic.

and resumed her Thursday Drawing Rooms at St James's, yet possibly never fully recovered her spirits (fig. 125). For the moment, she immersed herself in re-creating the lost world of Kew at her new country house, Frogmore, near Windsor. The royal family now took itself off on summer holidays to Weymouth and the King and some of the princesses began sea-bathing. All was not well, however. Tales of her sons' misdemeanours distressed the Queen. Her favourite son, the Prince of Wales, was constantly in debt and often at loggerheads with the King. There were tales of mistresses and illegitimate children. The princesses meanwhile were increasingly frustrated by their lack of any opportunity either to marry or to misbehave.

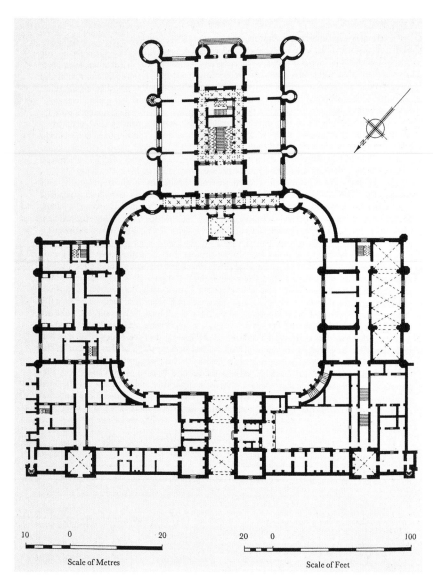

way for the works, and the White House was no longer maintained, thereby allowing rot to set in rapidly. The present Kew Palace was also probably earmarked for demolition. Building work was steady, but interspersed with bouts of the King's illness and other problems. In 1803, the King wrote to his daughter that "it advances but slowly", due, it seems, "partly to a certain lack of diligence in Wyatt and partly to the present lack of workmen", but the project was also consuming prodigious quantities of money. The initial £40,000 earmarked from the King's Privy Purse was woefully inadequate and by 1806 over £100,000 had been spent.

In every respect the building was a castle: fortress-like and brutal. A single plan and many romantic painted views survive (figs. 128, 130, 141), but there is only one passing reference to the interior and nothing descriptive. Entering a courtyard, the visitor was faced with a tall keep, receding as it grew in height immediately ahead, with high angular and corner turrets, all machicolated. There were high Gothic arches on the ground floor, but larger, square-headed windows on the first floor to the principal rooms. To the left and right were the east and west lodges, designed to house private apartments for the King and Queen. Documents suggest that the west lodge was never in fact built. Within the keep, however, a grand vaulted porch led through to a large entrance vestibule, with a magnificent grand stair of Portland stone beyond rising through the centre of the building, flanked by a succession of large state rooms and chambers.

128. Plan of the Castellated Palace, c. 1800. The north side, facing the river, comprised a grand and vaulted gatehouse, while a symmetrical exterior of turreted and castellated walls on either side concealed open courtyards and a warren of service rooms; the rear of the area changed in style to softer, circular turrets. The west 'lodge' was never built.

Wyatt, like Chambers before him, was the darling of the architectural world but far more versatile. On Chambers's death in 1796, Wyatt stepped naturally into his shoes as Surveyor-General. He had already brilliantly translated the Pantheon from Rome into its namesake in Oxford Street – a huge, domed, Neo-classical but commercial building used as a theatrical venue – but he was equally adept at the Gothic idiom, which had never entirely fallen out of fashion. He knew Horace Walpole's Strawberry Hill and had already designed Lee Priory near Canterbury, which showed his mastery of technique. Latterly he had excelled himself with the eccentric William Beckford's dizzy and exhilarating Gothic folly at Fonthill Abbey. It is not known whether the King pressed the style on Wyatt, or whether the architect expressed any preference himself.

The site of the new palace was chosen close to home. With Richmond Lodge now a memory and the focus of the estate concentrated at Kew Green, a decision was made to begin building close to the site of the White House, overlooking the river. The old Queen's House was probably pulled down to make

Though the building recalled ancient styles, possessing, as one observer noted, an air of sullen, solemn grandeur, in every other way it reflected modern planning and methods of architecture. It was an early iron-framed and -reinforced building, with walls of brick, covered with stucco and painted. This to some was in itself symbolic of degeneracy in architecture, which reflected badly on the King. Work was suspended following his final, permanent illness and isolation at Windsor.

Gaunt, empty and abandoned, it was summed up by Sir Nathaniel Wraxall in his *Reminiscences*, 1831, in a final word long after its demise as "a most singular monument of eccentricity and expense; though still unfinished and uninhabitable as it will probably ever remain, it presents to the eye an assemblage of towers and turrets forming a structure such as those which Ariosto or Spenser depictured princesses detained by giants or enchanters – an image of distempered reason".

Banks, the unofficial director

In the background, Sir Joseph Banks quietly and efficiently administered affairs in the gardens at Kew for the King. He organized the management of the merino sheep, maintained correspondence with travellers collecting seeds and plants for Kew from the new territories, and instructed William Townsend Aiton (who had succeeded his father, also William, as head gardener) on planting. In 1795, the Empress Catherine II of Russia desired a plant collection from Kew. Banks again was "just the man" to undertake this, appointing

the gardener to accompany the collection, selecting plants, which included *Strelitzia reginae* and *Fuchsia coccinea*, and to some extent financing the voyage to St Petersburg (fig. 129).

Recurrence of the King's illness

As the century drew to its close, Charlotte, Princess Royal, was the only one of the royal daughters to have escaped what was becoming increasingly referred to as "the nunnery" and was married to the Duke of Württemberg in 1797 (fig. 131). Desperate as she had been to leave, her chief delight now seemed to lie in evoking her childhood at her new home, requesting plants, seeds and even a pair of kangaroos to be sent from Kew. The Prince of Wales, separated from his new wife, whom he found unbearable, had neverthe-less managed to father a daughter, Charlotte. The young Princess was a great delight to her grandparents and her spinster aunts and was often invited to stay at Kew and Windsor. Princes and princesses got by as best they could: Edward, Augustus and Ernest pleading to be allowed to come home from overseas, the Prince of Wales and Adolphus begging to be sent abroad, the princesses languishing at home, apart from Princess Sophia (fig. 132), who under cover of "cramps" and "spasms" secretly gave birth to a boy fathered by the

King's middle-aged equerry, General Garth.

In February 1801, the King, while at the Queen's House in London, had a recurrence of his illness of 1788. Again the Willis doctors, led this time by the sons, Robert and John, were brought in and again Kew was recommended as an appropriate place for recuperation. The Duke of York and another Willis brother, Rev. Thomas, inspected the accommodation available for the King. The White House appeared all but derelict, "a cold house without even a chair in it, except what was in the room lately fitted up for the Prince Adolphus, and even some of the rooms without floors". They walked over the new Castellated Palace "and agreed that the situation was bad and the house itself not eligible". The only remaining house was Kew Palace, yet this too had its drawbacks, "being so overlooked that it could not by any means be advised to put the King into that. Neither independently of this objection could it be made convenient for the reception of the king in his present state." It was decided that the apartment prepared for Adolphus at the White House was the only possible option. The Queen approved but was fearful that the King should feel dread at being in the same apartments as he had occupied in his former illness.

LE TRIOMPHE DE L'AMOUR.

132. Princess Sophia in
c. 1800 by Henry Bone, 1806.
*The attractive fifth daughter
of George III was troubled
throughout her life with nervous
'spasms'. Like her sister Amelia,
she took the King's part against
her mother during his illness.
The King probably never found
out about her illegitimate son,
whom she rarely saw, but who
in later life badgered her for
money.*

from him. All these discussions, however, were overtaken by events. In mid-April, the Queen and the princesses moved to Kew Palace. The King, who had shown much improvement, but was by no means well, also rode to Kew and against the wishes of the Queen joined her there in the same house.

A posse of doctors and the Rev. Thomas Willis went to Kew on 20 April with the intention of putting the King again under their control and attempted to intercept him at the end of his morning ride. Having word during the day from the Queen that the King was "more quiet", the doctors stayed overnight at the Duke of Cumberland's house on Kew Green and resolved to ambush him the following morning. They failed and were obliged to go to Kew Palace and ask directly to see the King, who received them, with surprise and some anger, in his library. The doctors asked the King if they might see a picture of Van Dyck which was in the dining room, and, once they had him in this room, then spoke bluntly of the necessity of again putting him under their control. He replied, "I will never forgive you whilst I live", and made an attempt to leave the room but was stopped at the door by Dr John Willis with two of the men from the asylum. The King was told plainly "either he must remain in the house he then was and the Queen and family go to town, or they remain in the house and his Majesty go over to Kew [White] House into the apartments which were now occupied by Prince Adolphus". The King reluctantly agreed to the latter proposal. The Queen, all but broken by this new turn of events, submitted with mixed emotions to the imposed régime, employing Princess Elizabeth to liaise on her behalf with the doctors. All communication between the occupant of the White House and his family in Kew Palace some two hundred yards away was forbidden.

Yet the King seemed well enough to read and sign papers, and to take daily walks in the gardens, which invariably ended with a visit to Queen Charlotte's Cottage to see the kangaroos, now numbering eighteen. The Rev. Thomas Willis took it upon himself to be the sole means of communication with the new Prime Minister, Henry Addington, and Lord Chancellor Eldon, and this gave him power to manipulate events, a state of affairs he most relished. By 19 May, which happened to be the Queen's birthday, the King could tolerate the situation no longer and told Eldon that "he had made a solemn declaration that unless he was that very day allowed to rejoin the Queen and his daughters no earthly consideration should ever again induce him to sign his name to any state documents or to perform any act of kingly authority whatever". Once he was reunited with his family at Kew Palace, the King's health steadily improved and at the end of the month the royal family left for Weymouth.

Kew Palace is prepared for a visit

In November 1799, Kew Palace had been put into thorough repair, painted and fitted up with furniture from the White House, in obvious anticipation of a royal visit. John Vidler, the Works Mason, set up chimney pieces in the principal apartments and took down old marble water closets, while in the following year the joiner George Warren put in bookcases, shelves and a china closet. The freehold of the properties at Kew had finally been purchased by the King from the Countess of Essex in 1799. Rumours circulated that the King would now enlarge the White House, but the account of its derelict state, possibly affected by dry rot, lends weight to the supposition that the purchase of the freehold had been made in order to demolish the house, a process which was in fact begun in 1802. Wyatt's Castellated Palace was still not completed. Until it was habitable, only Kew Palace could offer stopgap accommodation. It is evident that the Queen and the princesses expected to stay at Kew Palace on their own for the period of the King's recuperation at Kew in 1801. The Queen, distressed by the King's visits to her apartments at the Queen's House in London, now professed herself too unwell to receive further visits

133. *The intertwining convolvulus and nasturtiums on the walls of the Picnic Room in Queen Charlotte's Cottage were very probably painted by Princess Elizabeth. She and Mary Moser, RA – a most accomplished flower painter – had already completed comparable wall decoration at Frogmore House in the grounds of Windsor Castle.*

RIGHT 134. *Princess Elizabeth's rooms were furnished with fashionable chintz in yellow and red. This example from 1804 has been used to re-create her Grecian couch and curtains.*

The King's illness returns a third time

Early in 1804, possibly precipitated by the stress of seeing his correspondence with the Prince of Wales published in the newspapers and with the threat of a French invasion still imminent, the King's health again gave way. This time he was treated by Dr Simmons of St Luke's Hospital and again it was proposed to move the King from London to Kew as soon as he was well enough. However, the King did not recover as before and for many months lingered in a condition "not ill enough to be shut up and not well enough to be left to his own guidance". He was still in this state in June when finally he removed to Kew where, to avoid the unpleasantness of the visit of 1801, rooms had been prepared for him in the eighteenth-century service wing of Kew Palace. Although in the same house, the King lived entirely separate from the Queen and dined with only his younger daughters, Sophia and Amelia. His apartments consisted only of a bedchamber, a small gallery hung with pictures and an adjoining dressing room that he used as a library. The Duke of Kent commented to the Prince of Wales that the King showed "a great coolness of manner towards our mother" and "an irritability that is not natural and his plans and schemes are without number ... I doubt if he knows himself what he means to do." The Queen was "ill and cross and the princesses, low, depressed and quite sinking under it". Princess Elizabeth, besides being once again the intermediary with the doctors, set to work ordering upholstery for Queen Charlotte's Cottage, where she probably began painting the charming nasturtium and convolvulus wall decorations (fig. 133).

The King's final visits to Kew

The King saw the Princess of Wales and his grand-daughter, Princess Charlotte, at Kew at the end of August 1805 before the royal family left for Weymouth again, where it became obvious that a cure had not been effected. The Secretary for War, Lord Hobart, wrote, "it is a melancholy circumstance to see a family that had lived together for such a number of years completely broken up". When it was time to leave Weymouth in October 1805, the family returned to the cramped quarters of Kew Palace while the princesses' apartments at Windsor were being refurbished. After two weeks, Princess Elizabeth sarcastically wrote to her brother, the Prince of Wales, "we are still at this beautiful chateau". Augusta added more philosophically, "although I am much better lodged at Windsor, we have such delightful rides and drives here". In fact Kew Palace had been put in order and the princesses' apartments richly furnished. George Pritchard, the bricklayer, rebuilt one of the east front gables, while repairs were made to shutters, sashes, mouldings and other elements in 1804. Princess Elizabeth's bedroom now contained a fashionable red and yellow draped Grecian couch and a set of six matching japanned Grecian chairs set

135. Princess Amelia in 1807 by Andrew Robertson, 1811. George III's favourite daughter, Princess Amelia, died of tuberculosis in 1810. She was deeply in love with the King's equerry, Charles Fitzroy, which she kept a secret to her death.

beneath a shallow recess (fig. 134). The sculptor Richard Westmacott installed a marble chimney piece with bronzed iron legs in the latest fashion. Augusta's rooms on the second floor were similar, with soft furnishings of maroon and yellow chintz, as were Amelia's next-door apartments, with a Gothic chimney piece. Princess Elizabeth planned a Sunday family outing to Queen Charlotte's Cottage where she had finished decorating; perhaps this was a conciliatory gesture to the King, but it was abandoned because of a heavy shower of rain. This turned out to be the King's last stay at Kew and probably he never saw his daughter's embellishments at the cottage.

Early in 1806, the King stopped off at Kew, as he had for so many years, to view progress on the estate. With costs having risen to an estimated £500,000, work was finally abandoned on the Castellated Palace. It was the end of the King's dreams for Kew.

Retirement to Windsor

As his Golden Jubilee approached in 1810, the King withdrew more often to Windsor, as did the Queen and, even more reluctantly, the still unmarried princesses. Princess Elizabeth unhappily commented, "we go on vegetating as we have done for the last 20 years of our lives". The youngest daughter, Amelia, however, was not vegetating but slowly dying from consumption (fig. 135). She begged to be allowed to return to Kew. Refurbishment took place at Kew Palace in 1809 with new carpets and curtains, card and work tables, firescreens and pier glasses, almost certainly in anticipation of this visit. The Queen, for whom Amelia had conceived a marked dislike in her sickness, thought it preferable for the Princess to be at Windsor, where she died a week after the King's jubilee on 2 November 1810.

It was perhaps this event that propelled the King into the final episode of his illness, from which, this time, there would be no substantial reprieve. From June of the following year, George III was never again seen outside the walls of Windsor Castle. Queen and daughters were equally imprisoned because of Charlotte's rigid view that the princesses' participation in any public event would show disrespect for the King. The Prince of Wales finally became Prince Regent in February 1811.

With the princesses, the Queen visited Kew in 1815 "for the benefit of the air", but this was the twilight of the reign and of royal Kew as tragedy and dispersal struck the royal family. The young Princess Charlotte, the hope of the dynasty and recently married to Prince Leopold of Saxe-Coburg, died after being delivered of a stillborn child (fig. 136). The nation was engulfed in grief as the potential heirs of two generations were in one sweep obliterated. The Queen lost her closest daughter and support when Princess Elizabeth, at the age of almost forty-eight, wed the unprepossessing Landgrave of Hesse-Homburg and moved to her husband's home, while Princess Mary married her cousin William, Duke of Gloucester.

Queen Charlotte's health was soon also giving cause for concern. On 22 June 1818 it was reported that she had "gone to Kew for a few days". From then on, her condition slowly deteriorated, often necessitating round-the-clock attendance by her physicians, at other times punctuated by slight recoveries of short duration.

A double wedding

Two more weddings were imminent in what was developing into a race to produce an heir to the throne.

Seven years earlier, William, Duke of Clarence, had parted from his "Little Pickle", the actress Dorothy Jordan, his common-law wife of twenty years and mother of his ten children. Failing to find an English heiress, he now proposed to marry, unseen, Princess Adelaide of Saxe-Meiningen. His younger brother, Edward, Duke of Kent, left his long-term French mistress for an official union with Princess Victoria of Saxe-Coburg. As Queen Charlotte was too ill to travel, the double wedding took place at Kew Palace, on 11 July 1818. The Queen's Drawing Room was fitted up with a temporary altar, an extended rail with four crimson velvet cushions to kneel on and a selection of the Chapel Royal's finest plate. The

136. *Princess Charlotte and Prince Leopold of Saxe-Coburg in their Box at Covent Garden Theatre, from the engraving by George Dawe, 1817. Princess Charlotte was the only daughter of George, Prince of Wales (later George IV) and Caroline of Brunswick. When she died giving birth to a stillborn son in 1817, the populace was grief-stricken. Although George III and Queen Charlotte had fifteen children, there were no other legitimate grandchildren until 1819.*

Archbishop of Canterbury conducted the service and the brides were given away by the Prince Regent. The Prime Minister, Lord Liverpool, the Lord Chancellor and Viscount Sidmouth made up the party. After the service the Queen retired to her private apartments and the wedding party was treated to a sumptuous meal in the downstairs dining room. The Duke and Duchess of Kent left for honeymoon at Claremont House in Esher, leaving the rest of the party to proceed in open carriages to Queen Charlotte's Cottage where they drank tea, while a twenty-one-gun salute was fired in the London parks and church bells rang throughout the City.

137. Morning Chronicle, Monday 16 November 1818. *Daily bulletins were issued from Kew Palace on Queen Charlotte's illness. By this stage it was apparent to all, except perhaps the Queen, that there could be no recovery. She died at Kew Palace on Tuesday 17 November 1818, in her seventy-fifth year.*

THE QUEEN.

The following are the Bulletins which have been received from Kew during the last week:—

"Kew-palace, Nov. 8.
"The Queen passed the evening of yesterday very uncomfortably, and has had a restless night; but there is no material alteration in her Majesty's symptoms.
"H. HALFORD."

"Kew Palace, Nov. 9.
"The Queen felt herself more easy throughout yesterday, but her Majesty's night has been a restless one.
"H. HALFORD."

"Kew Palace, Nov. 10.
"The Queen has not rested well in the night; but her Majesty has had some good sleep this morning.
"F. MILLMAN."

"Kew-palace, Nov. 11.
"The Queen has had a little sleep in the night, and her Majesty remains very much indisposed.
"F. MILLMAN,
"H. HALFORD."

"Kew-palace, Nov. 12.
"The Queen was in a less uncomfortable state throughout the whole of yesterday; but her Majesty has had a bad night.
"F. MILLMAN,
"H. HALFORD."

"Kew-palace, Nov. 13.
"The Queen had some sleep in the night; and her Majesty appears to suffer less to-day than she did yesterday.
"F. MILLMAN."

"Kew-palace, Nov. 14.
"The Queen continues in much the same state. Her Majesty rested ill in the early part of the night; but has had some good sleep this morning. "H. HALFORD."

In reference to the *actual* state of her Majesty, a Morning paper of yesterday publishes the following:—"It has been the constant observation of the public, that the bulletins from Kew have given very imperfect notices of the nature or progress of her Majesty's complaint. While rumour stated, from time to time, the private opinions of the Physicians, that the Royal Sufferer was fast approaching the universal doom—and that the certainty of a general mourning put a stop to all other manufactures, but that of articles in black; it was observed that no prayers were offered up to the Almighty in our churches for her recovery, nor was it understood that she had desired the spiritual consolation of any distinguished divine. Indeed, it was understood that her own confidence in her strength was at variance with the opinion of her Physicians. We have once or twice stated circumstances in her case, that came to our knowledge, differing essentially from the account of the Court Reporter. In like manner we now feel it our duty to state, that on Saturday evening last, her Majesty felt considerable temporary relief by a small rupture of the skin in both ankles, from which there has been since a considerable effusion of water. It was not occasioned by any puncture, but the effort of nature—and as we have stated, it had the effect of affording temporary relief; but it too frequently happens that such cracks in the skin of a dropsical patient produce symptoms of more speedy termination than the disease itself. We fear that her Majesty's malady is come to that stage when the most loyal, as well as filial tenderness, may pray for relief from her sufferings.—Her Majesty received the week before last a large packet of dispatches from the Duchess of Homburg, and we understand that a few days ago she gave orders to her silversmith to finish a sumptuous set of plate for a *dejeuné*, together with several articles of silk, as presents for her favourite daughter."—*Morn. Chronicle.*

The death of Queen Charlotte

The Queen was now confined to Kew. Her most ardent desire was to return to Windsor where the King was staying but normal carriage travel was out of the question. At the end of August she gave a dinner at Kew Palace to celebrate the birthday of the Duke of York and was well enough to join the royal party in the dining room for dessert, but shortly afterwards she suffered a relapse and from that date all thoughts of moving her were abandoned.

Kew Palace, it was observed, was not the ideal place for a royal invalid, the house being "unfit for royal residence in point of accommodation and most disadvantageously situated near the river". As the Queen's condition deteriorated, she kept mostly to her bedroom. A chair on rollers had been made for her to be wheeled into the boudoir where her dinner was served. The thoughtful Prince Regent, who visited her every day, had an ingenious reclining couch sent to his mother which provided a little relief. By mid-October the household at Kew had been reduced to a small retinue of servants and one set of carriage horses, with two horses saddled day and night for couriers ready to take out the news, which finally came on 17 November.

The Queen died in a chair in her bedchamber at Kew Palace just after 1 pm on that day. Her daughters Augusta and Mary were with her, while the Prince Regent and the Duke of York came immediately they were sent for and "instantly resorted to the chamber of their expiring parent who was perfectly sensible". Mary described those final moments: "We had the consolation of seeing her expire without a pang and a sweet smile on her face."

The state coffin lay in the bare, black-draped dining room under a canopy, lit by six candles in large silver candlesticks. Here, Lady Harcourt sat up the first night with the body of her friend of over forty years. Members of the royal household were admitted by ticket to file past the coffin. On the morning of 2 December, an honorary guard from the Brigade of Guards, with black crêpe and sashes, stood to attention outside Kew Palace and a detachment from the Sixteenth Lancers lined Kew Green as the hearse, covered with black velvet and decorated with ostrich plumes, was drawn by eight black horses escorted by eighty-nine Lancers in triple file. Even though the morning was cold, wet and dark, an immense crowd had turned out to witness Queen Charlotte's final leave-taking of Kew. The Queen finally, in death, reached Windsor. Thick straw had been laid down in the inner court of Windsor Castle to prevent the sound of the funeral carriages reaching the King's ears; the precaution proved to be unnecessary, his mind being absent.

George III died at Windsor on 19 January 1820.

After *Queen* Charlotte 1818–98

Following the death of Queen Charlotte, Kew Palace sinks into obscurity. Queen Victoria, unable to sell the palace, opens it to the public and it awakens new interest among the crowds of visitors to the increasingly popular Royal Botanic Gardens.

138. North Front, Old Palace from the Queen's Garden, *after George Ernest Papendiek, published 1820. This is one of the best views of the jumble of buildings erected to the west of the palace to house servants. The Castellated Palace looms in the background showing its close proximity to the palace.*

139. South view of Kew Palace *by John Buckler, 1827. One observer noted that "as this generation gradually passed away, the old mansion became more and more deserted; many of us remember it as it was a few years since, silent and ghostly, the blinds drawn, and without signs of life it might almost have been imagined that the Queen's corpse still lay within". The service wing to the left housed the rooms used by George III during his illness in 1804.*

The threat of destruction

In December 1818, *The Times* announced that the establishment at Kew Palace was to be broken up, leaving only the housekeeper and servants who had been there prior to Queen Charlotte's final visit. A report from Brighton a few days later "supposed it to be the Prince Regent's intention to make Kew Palace one of his principal summer residences", adding that the old palace and its outbuildings, long in a ruinous state, would be taken down and replaced by a new residence. It is unlikely that the Regent was ever serious about moving into the palace or indeed building a new one. A high wall and a screen of lofty evergreens were suggested to exclude the "unpicturesque" buildings of Brentford across the river. In reality Brentford had turned from a pretty fishing village of the mid-eighteenth century into a sprawling industrial town, whose soap and gas factories not only spewed smoke into the local atmosphere, but also filled the river with polluting effluent. No word was said of the King's monstrous folly, the Castellated Palace, which loomed over the site gaunt and unfinished.

Royal interest had not waned completely, merely shifted eastwards to Kew Green. In the first year of his reign, George IV (1820–30) purchased Hunter House and two adjacent houses on the north side (fig. 140). Before long, however, the King had lost interest or run out of money and the Kew estate was transferred to the Office of Woods and Forests, with charges for its maintenance borne by the Civil List.

The top end of the Green, which had been surrendered to the royal estate, was enclosed and a new entrance with two lodges made, on the understanding that more public access should be given to the pleasure grounds, but they remained open only on Sundays between midsummer and Christmas. The palace meanwhile was kept in good order. Benjamin Vulliamy oiled and repaired the clocks, and new papering and repainting occasionally took place, although a quantity of furniture was removed from Kew to Windsor. The old housekeeper, Mrs Tunstall, met a horrific death when her clothing was set alight by the open fire at her Kew lodgings. Her successor, Mary Murphy, continued to occupy the housekeeper's lodge, facing the palace, one of the surviving

 Early nineteenth-century mineral water bottle found buried near Kew Palace. Originating from Spa in modern Belgium, its iron-rich waters were tinted red and believed to have health-giving properties.

 In 1832, William IV erected a sundial on the site of the White House with an inscription recording the discoveries of the aberration of light and the nutation of the earth's axis made there by James Bradley in 1725.

 William Thiselton-Dyer was the son-in-law of Joseph Hooker and succeeded him as Director at Kew in 1885. He was a gifted botanist but his authoritarian stance on warders' uniforms caused problems among his staff.

140. George IV when
Prince Regent *by Sir Thomas
Lawrence, c. 1814. His over-long
wait for kingship made him
unfit for it. "There never was
an individual less regretted by
his fellow-creatures than this
deceased King", recorded his
obituary in* The Times *of
28 June 1830.*

early 1830s, as in June 1832 when Queen Charlotte's bedroom was papered, the attics were decorated and furniture was repaired in several rooms.

The fate of the Castellated Palace

By the late 1820s, and possibly in the course of further preparations to return to Kew, George IV finally resolved the fate of the Castellated Palace by ordering its destruction (fig. 141). Sir Richard Phillips, one of the few to glimpse its interior, described it as "a series of large closets, boudoirs and rooms like oratories. The foundation is a bog close to the Thames, and the principal object within its view is the dirty town of Brentford, on the opposite side of the river." In the summer of 1827, a Treasury order directed the transfer to the architect John Nash of "such of the materials of the … building as may be proper to convert towards the building of the King's Palace in St James's Park". Nash selected great quantities of oak and wainscot, pine boards, stone paving and Portland slabs to be removed in the first instance. Jeffry Wyatville, James Wyatt's nephew, was given permission to remove "all the windows and doors of the east wing for Windsor and all doors in the east and west towers". The remainder of the building was divided into lots for public sale and dismantling began. This was halted in December by the death of two workmen, when the speed of the work caused a section to collapse, taking masonry and scaffolding into the basement. Nevertheless, over half a million bricks, timber joists, ironwork and other building materials were carted away for recycling. In early 1828, Mr Aiton took "the vane complete with four large windows in the lanthorn" and the screen at the

group of residual buildings from the White House complex. Other servants included a porter, a turncock (a gatekeeper) and the housekeeper's servant, who lived in the service rooms to the west of the palace, where George III had been housed twenty years before.

In 1827, Robson & Co. rehung paper and canvas in the principal sitting room, bedroom, two other rooms and closets, Princess Mary's room and water closet, the grand staircase and the housekeeper's staircase. Similar refurbishment continued steadily into the

141. The Castellated Palace
*by Edward Goodwin
(fl. c. 1801–1816). It was
observed caustically and cruelly
that "this Anglo-Teutonic,
castellated, gothicized structure
must be considered as an
abortive production, at once
illustrative of bad taste and
defective judgement. From the
small size of the windows and
the diminutive proportion of its
turrets, it would seem to possess
windows that exclude the light
and passages that lead to
nothing." Another observer
dismissed it as "three dozen
turrets and towers".*

ing day. Finally, on 24 May, Princess Victoria of Kent was born, and just three days later a son, Prince George, was born to Ernest, Duke of Cumberland. The families of both the dukes of Cumberland and of Cambridge were to preserve their link to Kew by retaining houses on the Green.

In 1830, the Duke of Clarence, the third son of George and Charlotte, succeeded to the throne as William IV (1830–37) (fig. 142). He had a fondness for Kew, having lived for long stretches at Petersham and nearby Bushy, and less than two months into his reign he met the Surveyor-General of the Board of Works at Kew with a view to reoccupying Kew Palace. Following this, Wyatville was commissioned to design a major extension to the palace, which envisaged constructing a much longer wing in congruous architectural form and leaving the historic core as a simple extension to the new building. Drawings survive for the finished design (fig. 143), but the scheme came to nothing, and the architect's only long-lasting contribution to Kew Gardens was to be the small Classical King William's Temple, which still exists. The King returned the top section of Kew Green to the parish and further enlarged St Anne's Church, donating some of the pipes from a small organ that had been in the palace.

Kew Palace had by now been empty for almost fifteen years and there was little likelihood of renewed interest. Queen Adelaide was a regular visitor and in 1833 recalled seeing the chair in which Queen Charlotte had died "tied across with a piece of tape that no one might rest on it since she left it". Fanny Burney's niece, Charlotte Barrett, had gone especially to the palace a year after the Queen's death to see "Canaletto's Gallery", the collection of small Canaletto paintings bought early in George III's reign and transferred from the White House to the palace.

One of the first historians of the palace, John Heneage Jesse, recalled visiting the building at this time, perhaps with his father, who was Deputy Surveyor of the Royal Parks and Palaces and advised on the repair of the building. He found it almost untouched and its furnishings intact. He recalled, somewhat fancifully perhaps, the princesses' bed-chambers with white dimity bed curtains and simple furniture, a harpsichord, George III's favourite chair, a walking stick and a backgammon board. He also recorded seeing in a small room "the private prayer book of George III. In the prayer used during the session of Parliament, the King with his own hand had obliterated the words 'our most religious and gracious king' and had substituted for them 'a most miserable sinner'." By the early 1830s, however, orders were already being given for further removal of furnishings and pictures to the London palaces. Towards the end of his reign the King offered Kew Palace to his least favourite sister-in-law, the Duchess

142. William IV *by Sir David Wilkie, 1832. A bluff but kindly man, William was sent to sea at the age of fourteen. On his return he spent much time in and around Richmond with his actress mistress Dorothy Jordan and their ten children. When faced with marriage to the unknown Princess Adelaide at Kew, he wrote to his son, "She is doomed, poor dear innocent young creature, to be my wife." Yet it was a happy marriage and he made a popular king.*

base of the great stairs. By August, John Eversfield, the auctioneer, informed the Surveyor-General "that the taking down ... is very nearly completed, a very small portion of the building and foundation remains". Some of the final levelling may have been completed with explosives, and soon the King was "pleased to signify that the castellated house at Kew ... has been taken down".

The Green and the gardens

When George IV died in 1830, only seven of his siblings remained, but there were finally legitimate grandchildren to ensure the continuity of the dynasty. Prince Adolphus, Duke of Cambridge had produced a son in March 1819, and a short-lived daughter was born to Prince William, Duke of Clarence the follow-

143. Design for an extension to Kew Palace *by Sir Jeffry Wyatville, c. 1834. William IV flirted briefly with the idea of enlarging the palace. Wyatville's design comprised a new and slightly grander wing attached to the west of the existing building and extending southwards, in matching brick, which was broadly sympathetic. Like many before it, this proposal was soon abandoned. Wyatville's design was indeed modest and no plans survive.*

144. Princess Mary Adelaide of Cambridge, *later Duchess of Teck, aged twelve, by Richard James Lane, after Franz Xavier Winterhalter, 1846. The youngest daughter of the Duke of Cambridge spent much time at the family home of Cambridge Cottage on Kew Green, which she preferred to the family's elegant London house: "To exchange the green lawns and gardens of dear old Kew for that horrid London with all its smoke and dirt is too shocking to think of." She passed on her love of Kew to her daughter Mary, who became consort to George V.*

145. Adolphus Frederick, Duke of Cambridge *by James R. Swinton, 1846. The Duke of Cambridge was the most popular of the seven sons of George III to survive to adulthood. He spent his later years with his family in his London house or at Cambridge Cottage on Kew Green, where he was a well-known figure in the locality, an increasingly eccentric, but "charitable and popular" duke.*

of Kent. The Duchess refused it as "an old house quite unfit for the Princess [Victoria] and me to occupy, being very inadequate in accommodation and also almost destitute of furniture".

Royal links are retained

Royalty never entirely disappeared from Kew. The Cambridges made visits from Hanover, where, until the accession of his brother Ernest in 1837 as King of Hanover, Duke Adolphus served as Viceroy. When not at their house in Piccadilly, they returned to the comfort of Cambridge Cottage on Kew Green. Their son, Prince George, now had two sisters: Augusta, who married the Grand Duke of Mecklenburg-Strelitz, and the attractive Mary Adelaide (fig. 144), who married Prince Francis of Teck. Their eldest daughter, Mary, would one day become the queen of George V (1910–36) and exercise in turn a crucial influence on the palace. When the Cambridges returned to England in 1837, the house was enlarged with a new library, dining room and ground-floor drawing room looking into the gardens. The Duke of Cambridge, once George III's "little Dolly", became a well-known, eccentric character at Kew as he grew older (fig. 145). When he died in 1850 his body was brought to Kew for burial (fig. 146). When his son George in turn died in 1904, Cambridge Cottage was handed over to the emerging Royal Botanic Gardens.

Another son of George III retained close links with Kew. In 1806, Ernest, Duke of Cumberland had been given the house next to Cambridge Cottage, which had once been Lord Bute's study. William IV granted the Cumberlands the use of the larger Hunter House, originally purchased by George IV, which had become known as Royal Lodge. Often, on particular anniversaries such as their parents' birthdays, the surviving children of George III would meet for a *déjeuné* at Kew Palace followed by a drive through the

gardens and dinner. The Duke also retained a game preserve near Queen Charlotte's Cottage, and the use of the old deer park. On the death of William IV in 1837, his heir, the young Princess Victoria of Kent, under Salic law could not succeed to the crown of Hanover, and Ernest became King of Hanover, taking up permanent residence there. He later professed that his days at Kew had been "the happiest days of a long and turbulent life". Following his death in 1851, his home at Hunter House passed to the Royal Botanic Gardens and became the Herbarium.

The palace during the reign of Queen Victoria

Within a few years of Princess Victoria's accession to the throne in 1837, the remaining children of George III and Queen Charlotte were fast fading away, and the long-established family links with Kew weakened (fig. 147). The palace was all but forgotten and though it was never actually formally transferred from the Civil List, soon the Office of Woods and Forests began to care for it as it did the other redundant royal palaces. With the Queen's approval, the old White House kitchens were converted for the use of grace-and-favour residents, including Jane Sly, a former royal wet-nurse, given the job of looking after Queen Charlotte's Cottage, while Mary Murphy maintained her position as housekeeper. Voices were occasionally raised in protest at "the impropriety of keeping up the number of palaces for the royal family which the Queen never entered", but Kew continued to slumber in relative obscurity.

In 1838, a government report considered whether the royal gardens could provide the Queen with flowers and fruit as well as being open to the public, or whether they should be maintained solely as a scientific botanic institution. The findings were that a kitchen garden at Kew, enlarged with four acres from the Duke of Cumberland's land, could be main-

tained for the purpose of providing fresh produce for the London palaces and that the botanic gardens should be immediately transferred to the Office of Woods and Forests under trustees, with charges removed from the Civil List. The committee further expressed its opinion that the botanic gardens be "maintained on a scale creditable to the character of the nation and to the present state of Botanic Science in this country". They left the Treasury to determine who might pay for this. Under their first official director, Sir William Hooker, the botanic gardens began the initial, confident steps on their new, independent course and the essential relationship between the royal palace and its surrounding gardens was broken. Henceforth Kew Palace, which had been

the prime focus of the whole estate, became more and more subordinated as both a garden building and a public curiosity.

The last glimmer of the palace being used in its old way occurred in 1844 when Queen Victoria left her children, the Prince of Wales, the Princess Royal and baby Princess Alice, there for a short time to benefit from the country air. New inventories were already being made of the furnishings, however, with an eye to removal to other royal residences, and both the Office of Works, which replaced the Office of Woods and Forests, and Joseph Hooker, who succeeded his father, William, were hostile to this royal relic and the ongoing problem of maintenance. The old White House kitchens, now being used as accommodation, were condemned by the director, who wrote to the Office of Works in December 1845 complaining that "the buildings in question are not only incapable of being repaired to advantage, but ... their removal would be a decided improvement to the locality".

The palace, too, suffered from the depredations of subsidence and dry rot. The west wing, where George III had been confined, was a constant thorn in the side of the Office of Works. Later documents suggest that a deliberate decision was taken not to maintain it and from as early as 1848 there were complaints that the roof was decaying. It is probable that at this time, though documentary records are slender, severe structural problems were found in the south-east corner of the palace, necessitating what amounted to a partial dismantling and rebuilding. Identification of the brickwork shows substantial nineteenth-century repair work, strengthened by iron stanchions which were inserted between the window

piers and which came to light only in 1997 when panelling in the Queen's Drawing Room was removed. The roof was also rebuilt above the area. The west wing continued to plague the Office of Works through the 1870s. Finally, in 1880 a decision was made to dismantle this, an adjoining building and a privy shaft that had served the rooms on the west side of the palace. The work was carried out in the following year.

The modern botanic gardens are born

Despite the absence of royal occupants, the scientific and botanical interest stimulated by Princess Augusta and later George III was to have a profound effect on the development of the gardens in the nineteenth century, although they were now under the guidance of successive directors.

For a while after 1820 the future of the gardens looked uncertain. Aiton continued as best he could, but financial support declined and the administration and physical layout were relatively disorganized. By the end of the reign of William IV, George Glenny raged that "the state of the place is slovenly and discreditable, and that of the plants disgracefully dirty".

In a cost-cutting exercise undertaken by the government after the accession of Queen Victoria (1837–1901), the future of the gardens was mapped out. Following this, they were under threat of dissolution and closure, but a working party set up by the Treasury under the chairmanship of John Lindley, Professor of Botany at University College London, saw longer-term advantages to both science and the prestige of the country, and recommended that the area be developed as a scientific establishment.

The man appointed to fulfil Lindley's recommen-

148. Kew Palace and Outbuildings: Elevation of Servants' Offices, 1880. *A drawing prepared by the Office of Works for the demolition of the west range the following year.*

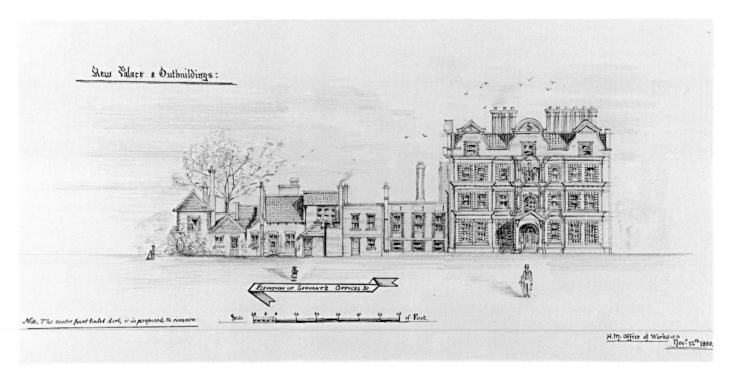

BELOW 151. *A London Transport poster by Fred Taylor, 1918, promoting the delights of Kew Gardens in the spring: a pleasant reminder of the peaceful diversions of rural Britain in a Europe that had been at war for four years. The expanding train and tram services brought a deluge of visitors to the gardens at Kew and the riverside at weekends.*

TOP 149. *The gradual disappearance of the great complex of royal buildings at Kew was charted in a series of maps in the eighteenth and nineteenth centuries. E. and G. Driver's map of 1840 follows an earlier example drawn up to assist John Lindley's working party in determining the fate of the gardens. By then, all trace of the White House and the Castellated Palace had disappeared.*

150. *The Palm House, designed by Decimus Burton and Richard Turner, was constructed between 1846 and 1848. It continued the tradition of innovative building at Kew, attracting large numbers of Victorian visitors eager to see new plants brought in from the farthest corners of the expanding British Empire.*

dations was Sir William Hooker, who succeeded William Aiton in 1841. Under Hooker the gardens were transformed, with donations of plant collections and specimens sent from an ever-expanding world and empire, together with new glasshouses and buildings for both storage and study. The public, too, began to flock to the gardens, particularly after the construction of the railway line to Richmond in 1846 and Brentford in 1853. By the middle of the century, with the construction of grand new designs such as the Palm House (fig. 150), the emphasis had tipped from the notion of a private pleasure ground to a major scientific institution and public recreation ground that belonged to the nation.

Two generations of Hooker, father and son, ensured the rise of the Botanic Gardens, with the founding of the Department of Economic Botany and Museums, Herbarium and library under Sir William and the building of the Jodrell laboratory in

1876 under Sir Joseph. Building on these foundations, the Royal Botanic Gardens at Kew evolved into what it is today: a scientific, botanic institution of world renown and influence in the study, preservation and protection of plant life throughout the world.

The Duke of Cumberland's land was eventually handed over to the Board of Works along with his former game reserve, but ownership of the land surrounding Queen Charlotte's Cottage and the gardens of Kew Palace along with the old White House kitchens and the site of the Castellated Palace proved to be an area of contention, centred on confusion as to who was responsible for the cost of maintenance.

The palace opens to the public

Towards the end of the nineteenth century it became increasingly clear that Kew Palace would no longer be suitable as a royal residence – a reality that needed to be acknowledged. Joseph Hooker noted that the

TOP 152. *Successive directors of the Royal Botanic Gardens cast eager eyes on the empty and shut-up palace, but Queen Victoria resisted all suggestions for an alternative use. This photograph of c. 1870 shows the Georgian porch, which was subsequently taken down.*

ABOVE 153. *The rustic qualities of Queen Charlotte's Cottage were accentuated by allowing ivy to grow unchecked, as seen here in this photograph of 1891. In 1887, in a rare event, the cottage was opened to the public to support a charity appeal at St Anne's Church, and was swamped by hordes of curious tourists.*

constant shunting of a railway goods yard across the river was a deterrent to any renewed royal interest and wrote asking if the palace could be used as a museum of forest specimens and crafts, to accommodate a growing collection of colonial timber. This plea fell on deaf ears. In the 1890s, the Duke of Cambridge asked the Queen if the house could be given to Lord Augustus Loftus, a retired diplomat and former governor of New South Wales, but this was also quietly refused.

In 1896, a survey of the palace pointed out that it was "totally unfit in its present state for a residence". Although in principle the Queen was against the sale of Crown property, she expressed an interest in selling several buildings including Kew Palace, as they had been unoccupied for so long. A proviso in the case of Kew Palace stipulated that it should be

bought by Kew Gardens and that the room in which Queen Charlotte had died should be left untouched. Ultimately, outright sale proved impossible, but the Queen approved of Kew Palace's transfer to the botanic gardens in return for the provision of a London residence for two of her children. A month later a memorandum was issued by the First Commissioner of the Board of Works, Mr Akers Douglas, to the effect that it was "also understood that the Queen will surrender the summer house, now known as the Queen's Cottage at Kew, together with the grounds for the purpose of being added to Kew Gardens". He commented, "the grounds of the Queen's Cottage amount to about 37 acres of very beautiful woodland. To open them to the public will be to add very greatly to the amenities of Kew", and would, he added, "considerably relieve the charge on the Civil List".

In January 1898 the office of housekeeper was dissolved and Kew Palace was handed over to be opened as a public museum. The rest should have been straightforward, but Hooker's son-in-law, the prickly William Thiselton-Dyer, now director of the gardens, had strong opinions which had not been reckoned with. There were two sticking points: one was that the character of the area around Queen Charlotte's Cottage would have to be greatly altered or damaged in order to provide full public access, and so it was agreed to fence off part of it. The second point seemed trifling: Thiselton-Dyer suspected that a Mrs Wheatstone, who lived at the Palace Lodge, was running a brothel. A threat to evict her evoked an appeal to the Duke of Cambridge, who considered that, given her advanced age, it would be unfair to leave her homeless, and the rector of St Anne's agreed. When Mrs Wheatstone then opened a teashop at the lodge, Thiselton-Dyer overstepped the mark. His intemperate remarks led the Board of Works to reconsider whether Kew Palace would be safe in his charge at all. To calm the situation, the board acted quickly and decisively and by April the palace had been transferred to the charge of its own surveyor, who appointed a warder so that the building could be opened to the public in time for the Queen's birthday in May (fig. 154).

A *Hundred* Years *of* CHANGE

Kew Palace undergoes changes in its public displays throughout the twentieth century. Archaeological research and greater understanding guide a major re-presentation in the twenty-first century, which re-creates a setting George III would recognize.

A new public attraction

On 24 May 1898, Kew Palace opened to the public. In reality it was little more than an empty building but the gift of the Queen attracted considerable attention. The reign of George III was almost beyond recall, but many of the first visitors to the palace had direct links to the period through their parents or grandparents, and it was recognized from the outset that Kew had a special affinity with King George and Queen Charlotte. The era of sophisticated displays in historic houses lay far in the future, but attention was given almost immediately to the presentation of the interior. Most of the ground- and first-floor rooms were initially bare and Percy Fitzgerald, who gave Queen Victoria a large collection of prints and pictures, noted that the appearance of the palace was poor, enlivened only by "lean and dingy bits of embroidery". Several pieces of furniture were returned, including the armchair in which Queen Charlotte had died, some chairs, sofas and clocks, which were arranged around the

Ritual protection marks were discovered on the roof timbers of Kew Palace in 2004. They were carved by the palace's superstitious occupants in the 1630s to ward off evil spirits or witches.

Modern archaeological techniques have revealed the figure of a woman, part of a painted scheme dating from the seventeenth century in the King's Library.

The violent storm in March 1916 that destroyed the Temple of the Sun also blew down the last of the Seven Sisters elms, reputedly planted by the daughters of George III.

edges of several rooms and protected by rope barriers. A portrait of George III was despatched from Hampton Court Palace in 1899 and the following June a list was drawn up of pictures to be transferred from Windsor, including paintings by Sebastiano Ricci, flower pictures by Baptiste and some "foreign birds" by Bogdani. The influential Sir Spencer Ponsonby-Fane, Comptroller of Her Majesty's Household (fig. 157), devised a 'Flora Room' in the Queen's Boudoir, where Ricci's *Triumph of Flora* could be accompanied by pictures of flowers to create a miniature gallery. (A guidebook was also produced by Ernest Law, the Hampton Court curator, and published in 1905.) The palace was open all year round, with free entry, and was patrolled by a single warder.

The area around the palace including the old White House kitchens was retained by the government as workshops and accommodation for the Clerk of Works. The area forming the site of the demolished Castellated Palace and the garden to the north of the palace, which had always been a gentle sloping lawn down to the river, was put to use as a vegetable garden. Immediately to the south-west of the palace, Chambers's clock tower had probably been demolished with part of the stable block in the 1850s. In 1905 the remaining stable buildings were pulled down. This was all part and parcel of a gradual denuding of the gardens that George III would have recognized, which continued throughout the later nineteenth and the early twentieth century. Temples were rebuilt in stone, or demolished and replaced by new, botanical structures such as greenhouses, new museums, lodges and planting, as the emphasis on botany gradually

supplanted the character of royal pleasure ground. The Orangery became a museum of timber and in 1916 Chambers's Temple of the Sun was crushed under a falling tree, and its ruins unceremoniously swept away (fig. 159).

Renewed interest, 1925–35

The 1920s were a time of both increasingly popular mass tourism and a revival of royal interest in the buildings at Kew. A tangible link with the Georgian royal family was maintained by Queen Mary, consort of George V, who was herself the great-granddaughter of George III. Her grandparents (Adolphus, Duke of Cambridge, and the Duchess of Cambridge) and her mother Mary Adelaide, Duchess of Teck, had lived on the Green and were buried in a specially built mausoleum at St Anne's. (In the 1930s Queen Mary had the coffins removed to the royal burial ground at Windsor.) Queen Mary spent many years re-acquiring for the Royal Collection many personal pieces and possessions which had been disposed of or given away by George III and Queen Charlotte to courtiers and family members, or sold on the Queen's death in 1818. In early February 1925, Mary visited Kew, ostensibly to select some flower paintings to be transferred to her new flower room at Frogmore, but she also renewed her interest in the displays. Though she took the very paintings that made Kew attractive to the public, her firm opinion was that the palace should be decorated by items of furniture and paintings that had a direct relevance to her Georgian forebears, and she responded to the implied criticism by sending six large Bogdani flower and game paint-

157. Sir Spencer Ponsonby-Fane (1824–1915), a satirical portrait by the caricaturist Leslie Ward, known as "Spy". Fane was Comptroller of the Queen's Household and was influential in the opening of Kew Palace to the public. He took an active interest in the early public displays there.

158. The Queen's Drawing Room, c. 1920. In the early twentieth century, a few pieces of furniture were scattered throughout the house, but several rooms remained empty. Where original paintings were not available, prints showing George III and his family were hung on the walls. Note the marble chimney piece that survives from 1631; resembling contemporary tomb sculpture, it was carved from black Tournai marble and alabaster to give a rich effect.

4. KEW PALACE, QUEEN'S DRAWING ROOM.

ABOVE 159. *William Chambers's Temple of the Sun was crushed by a falling cedar on 28 March 1916. Careful maintenance had preserved the temple, unlike most of its companions, and it had not been rebuilt in the nineteenth century.*

ABOVE RIGHT 160. *Queen Mary visiting Kew in 1947. Queen Mary, wife of George V and granddaughter of the Duke of Cambridge, took a great interest in her great-grandmother, Queen Charlotte, and the old family homes at Kew.*

ings from Windsor to be hung on the staircase. Though redecoration was undertaken periodically, by the early 1930s it was acknowledged that the palace was decidedly old-fashioned in style and had little appeal. Sir Lionel Earle, Permanent Secretary of the Office of Works, began to correspond with the Victoria and Albert Museum. "The Lord Chamberlain", he revealed, "has been writing to me about the dullness and unattractiveness to the public of the little old Royal Palace in Kew Gardens." He recognized that "the house can never be really interesting to the public until there is a modicum of eighteenth-century furniture in it", and tentatively asked for any attractive

furniture that the museum could provide.

In 1932 a concerted effort was made to freshen up the displays. A number of requested items were forthcoming from the Victoria and Albert Museum, as well as the Royal Collection. Prince Frederick's harpsichord, which had firm links to the palace but had languished in obscurity at Windsor since being removed in 1875, was returned after protracted negotiations. Some rather drastic redecoration was undertaken. Ernest Law had first recommended the stripping of the oak panelling in the King's Breakfast Room and his suggestion was now revisited (fig. 161). In June 1932, the many layers of paint were

161. *An early twentieth-century view of the King's Breakfast Room. Until 1932, the seventeenth-century panelling in this room was painted white. This was removed in the mistaken belief that the original timber was always meant to be exposed. In fact analysis of minute traces shows that this paint had a long history.*

162. The north elevation of Kew Palace during the restoration of the garden in 1969. This land had been used to grow vegetables ever since the embanking of the River Thames and levelling of the area in the early twentieth century. The demolition of the earlier loggia in the nineteenth century had left the building with no northern entrance.

stripped and burned off, revealing a patchwork of oak and pine repairs, which were then grained to give the room the dark oak appearance it retains to the present day. The stone colour of the window architraves was changed to white under the mistaken impression that this was authentic. A new guidebook was published by R.S. Simms, and a second full-time warder was appointed. For the first time, an entry charge was applied, and it was proposed to close the palace during the winter.

Queen Charlotte's Cottage

The cottage meanwhile had undergone some changes since its transfer to the Office of Works. Mr Thiselton-Dyer happened to be walking towards the Wilderness in 1901 when he noticed a cloud of smoke. On investigating, he discovered that the cottage was being rethatched; the old thatch was being burnt and replaced with straw instead of the traditional reed, and without any consultation with him. The original tone and colour, which were calculated to enhance its charm, were now destroyed and he raged in a letter that "the roof has now no more attractiveness than a haystack". Thus began a long period of repair and wrangling over cost. The thatch was patched in 1914 and again in 1916, when the use of tarpaulin was mooted. During the Second World War the cottage suffered blast damage to its windows and ceilings, and a question was asked by the local Member of Parliament whether the building could

be modified to house families displaced by the bombings in London. It was pointed out that the cottage had no amenities or electricity, and the proposal was dropped. Wartime damage then needed to be made good and attention turned to the better presentation of the building. In 1950 the roof was rethatched with Norfolk reed and the building was prepared with chintz curtains and items of furniture transferred from the palace. Bluebells and narcissi were planted round about the area in order to enhance its appearance and in 1959, to celebrate the bicentenary of Princess Augusta's botanic garden, the cottage was opened to the public.

The 1967–76 re-presentations

During the 1950s, attempts were made to improve the appearance of Kew Palace beyond general maintenance and the displays were enhanced with new loans. In 1954 John Charlton, Inspector of Ancient Monuments, sourced from the Royal Collection more items closely associated with George III.

The 1960s represent an important time for Kew Palace for, once again, attention turned to the appearance of the building, which still preserved much of the spartan drabness of the late Victorian displays. Care of the palace had devolved from the Office of Works to the Ministry of Public Buildings and Works in 1962, soon (in 1970) to be absorbed into the new Department of the Environment (DoE). Works at the palace had begun in 1967. To the north the gardens,

RIGHT 163. *Queen Elizabeth II visiting the Queen's Garden in 1969. Ten years earlier, Her Majesty The Queen had visited Kew to unveil a new dial fitted to an earlier sundial to mark the bicentenary of the Royal Botanic Gardens.*

FAR RIGHT 164. *The external brickwork of the palace has been patched and repaired many times. The most ambitious alterations occurred in 1967–69 when the Classical loggia was re-created at the rear of the palace (see fig. 165).*

165. *The Queen's Garden is presented as a late seventeenth-century garden using only plants that were available in England before 1700. It incorporates the terms that had belonged to Frederick, Prince of Wales at Kew, a fountain with a cast Verrocchio putto, a gazebo and a piece of ironwork by Tijou discovered in the 1930s in the Home Park at Hampton Court.*

which had traditionally been a sloping lawn with a line of elms, were levelled when the River Thames was embanked. The area subsequently languished as a vegetable garden. In 1969 it was transformed with the creation of the Queen's Garden (fig. 162). This was designed by Sir George Taylor, then Director of the Royal Botanic Gardens, in a late seventeenth-century style, using plants that were available in cultivation only before 1700, with a camomile lawn and box hedges in front of the palace (fig. 165). The gardens were also adorned with Prince Frederick's terms, a Venetian well-head and fragments of late seventeenth-century ironwork by Jean Tijou reworked into a decorative pillar (fig. 163). At the same time the palace was put into good order, with structural modifications. The arcaded loggia on the north side, which had disappeared in the nineteenth century, was reconstructed on the lines of archival drawings and illustrations, thereby restoring a north door and grand entrance to the house (figs. 164, 165). Elsewhere, missing elements were reinstated.

Within the DoE, the care of the unoccupied royal

palaces fell to the Directorate of Ancient Monuments and Historic Buildings, with the maintenance undertaken by the Property Services Agency (PSA). Under the direction of the senior architect, Harold Yexley, new interiors were installed between 1973 and 1976, comprising displays devoted to George III and his family in the Pages' Waiting Room (fig. 166) and other ground-floor rooms, while the first floor was redecorated in Georgian style, with fabrics and decorative items designed by Pamela Lewis, then Yexley's architectural assistant, using period wallpaper patterns and muted fawn, white and grey colours. The Queen's Boudoir was given a yellow stripe decoration, while the so-called King's Bedroom (later discovered to be Princess Elizabeth's bedroom) had black and scarlet wallpaper (fig. 168) and the Queen's Bedroom was adorned with blue – all provided by the firm of Cole and Son with French papers by Percheron. John Charlton, with Oliver Millar, Surveyor of The Queen's Pictures, chose new schemes for the corridors and the stairs. Some relics

of the earlier schemes, such as the dark papier-mâché furniture crammed into the Queen's Antechamber, did, however, stay (fig. 170).

New furniture was provided with loans from the Royal Collection and the Victoria and Albert Museum. As before, the Tschudi harpsichord formed a centrepiece in the Queen's Drawing Room, which had now been given a slightly French feel with gilding on the panelling; new paintings of George III, the Queen and their children brought something of the eighteenth century back to the palace. A bed was refurbished for the Queen's Bedroom from lengths of carved bamboo in store at the Victoria and Albert Museum, previously part of an earlier Chinese-style bed. In June 1976, the palace finally reopened to the public. It evoked the Georgian era of cool colours, style and elegance, but the scheme was not entirely faithful to the original appearance of the house.

Visitor numbers rose from this time, as the palace became a popular adjunct to the gardens, but the new displays were to last only twenty years. Structural

166. The Pages' Waiting Room was originally divided into smaller closets for musicians and the King's pages. By the 1970s, it contained a display of personal items from the family of George III assembled by Pamela Lewis and later housed a small shop.

TOP 167. *Documentary research and archaeological analysis have been used to re-present Princess Elizabeth's bedroom as it may have appeared in c. 1804. The green verditer wallpaper is hand-made and fringed with a flock border, while the sumptuous textiles and carpets are rewoven from historic designs.*

ABOVE LEFT 168. *Princess Elizabeth's bedroom before re-presentation. From around 1905, this room was erroneously known as the King's Bedroom. In the 1960s, its rather plain walls were decorated with heavily patterned black and scarlet wallpaper.*

ABOVE RIGHT 169. *Removal of the 1960s decorative scheme in Princess Elizabeth's bedroom revealed a treasury of complex archaeological features, which had been neither commented on nor recorded during previous refurbishments. Traces of earlier coving, structural elements and finishes were laid bare for the first time.*

problems emerged once again in the 1980s. Earlier problems had been found in the undercroft, where the plaster ribs of the vaulting had been stripped of render in the late 1960s and the bricks repaired, but in 1986, a structural survey revealed far more alarming decay, with extensive cracking in the brickwork and problems in the floor joists. This was rectified, but provided only a temporary stopgap. In the late 1980s, there were even proposals to refurbish the second floor, which had been little touched since 1818, as offices for the PSA. Thankfully, to more conservation-minded eyes, these came to nothing.

Historic Royal Palaces

Under the National Heritage Act of 1983, a new body, English Heritage, was created to care for the state-controlled Ancient Monuments and Historic Buildings but Kew Palace and Queen Charlotte's Cottage were not included and remained in the care of the DoE. In 1989, however, an executive agency, the Historic Royal Palaces Agency, was established to care for the five unoccupied royal palaces – the Tower of London, Hampton Court Palace, Kensington Palace State Apartments, the Banqueting House in Whitehall and Kew Palace with Queen Charlotte's Cottage. The Agency was transformed into a non-departmental government body with charitable status in 1998 and government funding for Kew Palace, which had formed a perennial source of conflict and confusion, was finally ended. Henceforth,

the costs of maintenance and conservation of the palace would be borne solely by Historic Royal Palaces from its own revenues and charitable fund-raising activities.

Kew Palace today

The 1980s building repairs were precursors to a much more drastic period of stabilization, begun when large cracks were discovered in the walls of the Queen's Bedroom in the mid-1990s. Several of the displays needed to be dismantled for the damage to be investigated, but a second, thorough survey revealed a catalogue of severe problems in the brickwork of the gables and in the walls, decay in the timbers, and the disengagement of the internal floor joists as the outer walls spread, which needed immediate attention. In 1996, the decision to close the palace was taken as the onset of decay threatened the collections. The furniture and paintings were returned to their respective owners or put into store and the first phase of repairs began. While these stabilized the structure and allowed comprehensive rewiring at a cost of £1.5 million, they also provided a unique opportunity for Historic Royal Palaces to understand more about the building. The palace is a Grade I Listed building and Scheduled Ancient Monument enjoying the highest level of protection, so that permission for intrusive investigations is under normal circumstances only rarely given by English Heritage. However, the repairs necessitated the dismantling of

ABOVE LEFT 171. *Rooms laid bare, 1990s. The careful removal of extensive areas of panelling and flooring revealed massive joists and seventeenth-century brickwork in the building for the first time. The Queen's Drawing Room is typical of many rooms exposed in this way.*

ABOVE RIGHT 172. *Important decorative features such as graining have been reinstated at Kew. Plain doors are given an oak-grained effect, using traditional techniques and materials, which have changed little in two hundred years.*

RIGHT 173. *Many of the early nineteenth-century paint colours have been reinstated in the palace based on an extensive programme of paint analysis. Small samples of paint were examined in cross-section to reveal successive layers and colours. Some rooms have up to twenty-two layers of paint, interspersed with evidence of varnish and even deposits of soot and grime from open fires.*

174. *Fragments of Greek key border in green with black flock found in Princess Amelia's bedroom and replicated for the re-presentation of the palace in 2005.*

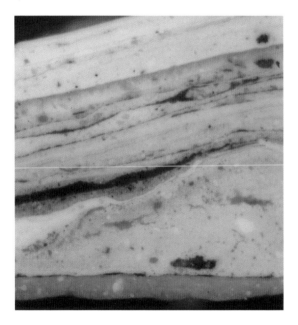

large areas of panelling, the lifting of floorboards and the removal of the 1960s fibreboard wall coverings, exposing much of the internal skeleton of the building and providing a unique opportunity for investigation (figs. 169, 171). Relatively new archaeological techniques such as ground-penetrating radar and rectified photography were used, all of which served to enhance knowledge of the building. Architectural surveys identified ritual protection marks, first applied to the roof timbers in the seventeenth century as a means of warding off evil spirits. Even during the final stages of the project, fresh discoveries of wall paintings continued to provide a new and fascinating perspective into the history of the building (fig. 21).

A comprehensive programme of paint analysis was undertaken, which enabled the decorative history of the palace to be unravelled for the first time (fig. 173). Hundreds of scraps of wallpaper were uncovered, including fragments of early nineteenth-century green 'verditer' with flock paper borders, chrome yellow papers and patterned Victorian designs (fig. 174). A small piece of the verditer removed for conservation preserved, almost miraculously, an identification stamp or frame-mark that placed it securely in the year 1804. During the investigations, it became clear that the twentieth-century redecorations had progressively eroded the integrity of the building and that it bore little resemblance to the form in which George III would have known it. This inspired Historic Royal Palaces to begin the process of designing a new and more authentic re-presentation that

175. *Queen Charlotte's Bedroom after re-presentation in 2006. The bed has simple white dimity hangings in stark contrast to the princesses' colourful beds. To the right is the chair in which the Queen is reported to have died in 1818.*

would reflect both the best surviving physical evidence and the moment when the palace took centre stage in the nation's affairs, during the illness of the King. A thorough documentary reappraisal of the building was undertaken, which threw up several surprises. It revealed some misidentification of the rooms, for example. The room previously known as the King's Bedroom was probably used instead by Princess Elizabeth in the early 1800s, while that used by George III himself had lain in the demolished west wing. Research revealed that the early nineteenth-century decorative schemes had been colourful, with a sandy pink shade on the joinery, green verditer wallpapers throughout the first floor, and fitted carpets. In 2005, the previously restored parts of the house were prepared along the lines of its appearance around 1804. Doors were regrained (fig. 172), colours restored as closely as possible to their original tones and hand-made wallpapers rehung using traditional methods, with canvas lining. The intention was not to give a pristine appearance to all the interiors, but instead to combine greater authenticity with the right feel and atmosphere of a house occasionally occupied by the royal family (fig. 175). New displays were installed, illustrating the life of George III and Queen Charlotte at Kew, while, for the first time, the whole story of the house was threaded through the new interpretation, culminating in the revelation of the second floor: a unique and untouched space that had never been opened to the public before and has changed little since last occupied by the royal princesses in 1816 (fig. 177).

Today, Kew Palace appears very different from how it was at any period within living memory, but it is at the same time a reflection of pioneering and

176. *The bathing machine at Weymouth "puts me in mind of the baby house we had at Kew", wrote Princess Mary to George III. Now an exhibit at Kew Palace, this dolls' house was made by the princesses for the children of Captain Grey, captain of the King's flagship at Weymouth. The interiors and furnishings of the little house bear a striking similarity to the decoration and furniture at Kew Palace at the beginning of the nineteenth century.*

occasionally controversial conservation solutions to similar buildings. During the external repairs, traces of an original coloured wash were discovered preserved beneath a rainwater pipe, and Historic Royal Palaces took the decision in 1999 to restore a traditional limewash coloured with ochre, which reflects the appearance of the palace in its early days and subsumes the patchwork of brick repairs beneath the architectural lines and elements (fig. 178). The stark white colour of the window surrounds has been banished and replaced with authentic, warmer tones. A pressing issue was to provide level access to the principal floors, and so the viability of installing a lift was explored. Records showed that a privy or lavatory shaft had once risen above the roof of the demolished west wing, and examination revealed that a lift could be built on its site that would broadly echo its form and scale. In 2005, an entirely reversible solution was provided by a steel-framed lift shaft, clad in weathered oak; the plinth of the main door was raised and Portland stone ramps installed.

The palace stands today secured for future generations. As well as being an architectural gem of the highest importance, it is also the only residence that George III would recognize today, were he to return to the tranquillity of Kew Gardens. There have, however, been many changes. Almost all of his garden buildings have disappeared, while the Physick and Flower gardens, which formed the core of botanical study, have been superseded by the slow development of an institution devoted to science, of which he would undoubtedly have approved. Of the great royal complex of palaces and buildings developed by his grandmother and parents, Kew Palace remains a central focus. Moreover, if the King could look out from the Queen's Drawing Room today he would see other familiar friends. The Orangery survives, the kitchens that once served his food and, nearby, a tree planted by his daughter Augusta, which lives yet.

ABOVE 177. *The second floor of the palace provides a unique view of an interior little touched by time. Princess Augusta's bedroom preserves its late eighteenth- or early nineteenth-century painted panelling and floorboards, marred only by some mischievous graffiti drawn during the 1960s. The room would have been embellished with textiles, wall-hangings, carpets and elegant furniture.*

RIGHT 178. *Traditional 'ruddling' or 'russeting' was once common and involves applying a coat of pigment or limewash over the brickwork. This is sacrificial and will wash off with time. Archaeological analysis revealed that Kew Palace had originally been treated in this way and the limewash was reapplied in 1999.*

FURTHER READING

Many books on Kew have been published over a number of years. For a brief, illustrated look at the wider area, a starting point would be David Blomfield's *Kew Past*, published in 1994 as part of a series of informative local books by Phillimore. The magisterial study of Kew and neighbouring Richmond remains John Cloake's *Palaces and Parks of Richmond and Kew*, published by Phillimore in two volumes in 1995 and 1996 and the result of many years of detailed historical research. Finally, Ray Desmond's *Kew: The History of the Royal Botanic Gardens* (The Harvill Press, 1995) forms a compendious view across the fascinating history of the gardens.

ACKNOWLEDGEMENTS

The authors and publishers would like to thank all those members of the staff of Historic Royal Palaces and others who have contributed in any way to the preparation of this book. Particular thanks are due to Sebastian Edwards, David Souden and Lucy Worsley for advice on the draft text. Many thanks are also due to the staff of the Royal Botanic Gardens, Kew; to Robin Wyatt and Jonathan Foyle for providing illustrations; to Annie Heron for procuring at times almost unobtainable images in order to give the book a fresh look; and to Clare Murphy, Historic Royal Palaces' Publications Manager, for managing the project, editing the text and making many valuable suggestions.

Historic Royal Palaces gratefully acknowledges the permission of Her Majesty Queen Elizabeth II to make use of any previously published material from the Royal Archives that still falls within copyright.

INDEX

PICTURE CREDITS

First published in 2006 by Merrell Publishers Limited

Head office:
81 Southwark Street
London SE1 0HX

New York office:
49 West 24th Street, 8th Floor
New York, NY 10010

merrellpublishers.com

in association with

Historic Royal Palaces
Hampton Court Palace
Surrey KT8 9AU

hrp.org.uk

Text copyright © 2006 Historic Royal Palaces
Pictures copyright © 2006 the copyright holders (see left)

British Library Cataloguing-in-Publication data:
Groom, Susanne
    Kew Palace : the official illustrated history
    1.Kew Palace (Richmond-upon-Thames, London, England) – History
    I.Title II.Prosser, Lee
    728.8′2′0942195

    ISBN 1 85894 323 X

Edited by Clare Murphy and Elisabeth Ingles
Indexed by Hilary Bird
Designed by Maggi Smith

Printed and bound in Slovenia

HALF TITLE: *Kew Palace, 2006.*

FRONTISPIECE: *A London Transport poster by Fred Taylor, 1918, promoting the delights of Kew Gardens in the spring.*